O-Parts HUNTER

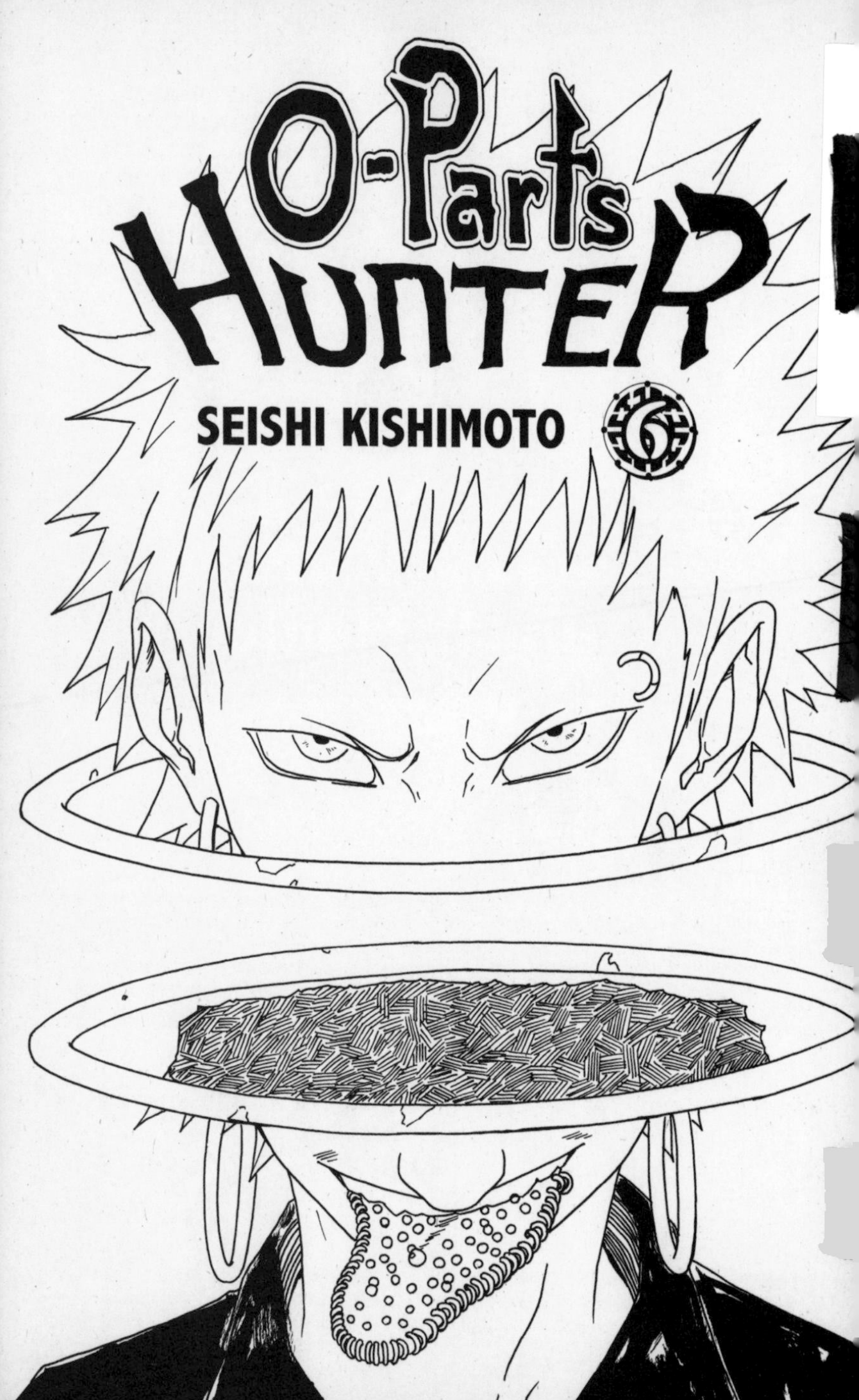
O-Parts
HUNTER
SEISHI KISHIMOTO
6

LET HIM THAT HATH UNDER-STANDING COUNT THE NUMBER OF THE BEAST: FOR IT IS THE NUMBER OF A MAN; AND HIS NUMBER IS...
666
REVELATION 13:18
A VERSE OUT OF THE *NEW TESTAMENT*

O-Parts Hunter

SPIRITS
O-PARTS

Spirit: A special energy force which only the O.P.T.s have. The amount of Spirit they have within them determines how strong of an O.P.T. they are.

O-Parts: Amazing artifacts with mystical powers left from an ancient civilization. They have been excavated from various ruins around the world. Depending on their Effects, O-Parts are given a rank from E to SS within a seven-tiered system.

ECT

O.P.T.

Effect: The special energy (power) the O-Parts possess. It can only be used when an O.P.T. sends his Spirit into an O-Part.

O.P.T.: One who has the ability to release and use the powers of the O-Parts. The name O.P.T. is an abbreviated form of O-Part Tactician.

Jio Freed
A wild O.P.T. boy whose dream is world domination! He has been emotionally damaged by his experiences in the past, but is still gung-ho about his new adventures! O-Part: New Zero-shiki (Rank B)
Effect: Triple (Increasing power by a factor of three)

Ruby
A treasure hunter who can decipher ancient texts. She meets Jio during her search for a legendary O-Part.

Satan
This demon is thought to be a mutated form of Jio. It is a creature shrouded in mystery with earth-shattering powers.

STORY

Ascald: a world where people fight amongst themselves in order to get their hands on mystical objects left behind by an ancient civilization...the O-Parts.

In that world, a monster that strikes fear into the hearts of the strongest of men is rumored to exist. Those who have seen the monster all tell of the same thing – that the number of the beast, 666, is engraved on its forehead.

***

Jio, an O.P.T. boy who wants to rule the world, travels the globe with Ruby, a girl in search of both a legendary O-Part and her missing father. When the two reach Entotsu City, a town crushed under the heel of government oppression, they find that the governor, Jaga, has been tricked by Wise Yury, the Crimson Magician, into activating Mexis, an O-Part of mass destruction! The townspeople trust Jio and support him in his struggle to protect them against this evil...but they have no idea of the sinister force that Mexis has awakened in Jio!

O-Parts Hunter

Table of Contents

ZCH
DAMN IT, THE STUPID TOWN LABORERS ARE RUNNING WILD!!
AND WHERE DID THOSE BRATS GO?!
HUH, DON'T MESS WITH US KIDS FROM THE RESISTANCE MOVEMENT.
BY THE TIME YOU FEEL A CHILL DOWN YOUR BACK, IT'S TOO LATE.
BONNNNK
CRAK
SMAK
WHAK
WELL DONE, TANUKI!!
YUP...
WHAT IS THIS STRANGE FEELING ...?

CHAPTER 23: ARCHENEMY

SP

GGGG

GGGG

KSSSSSH

GRP

WHAT HAPPENED?
MEXIS IS A MESS... IT'S GOING TO TAKE A LITTLE LONGER TO REGENERATE.

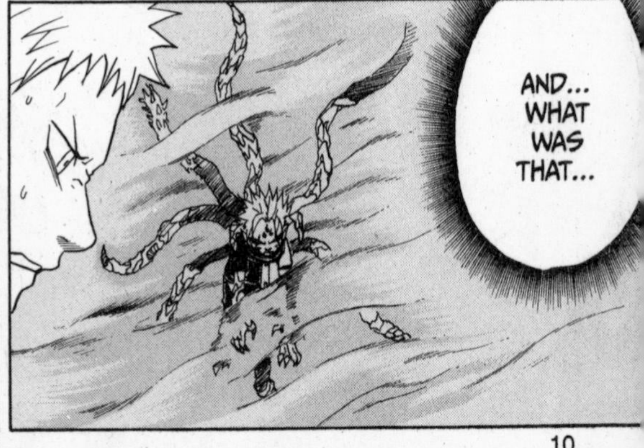
AND... WHAT WAS THAT...

IS THAT YOU... BROWNY?
SP

SWIK
!!

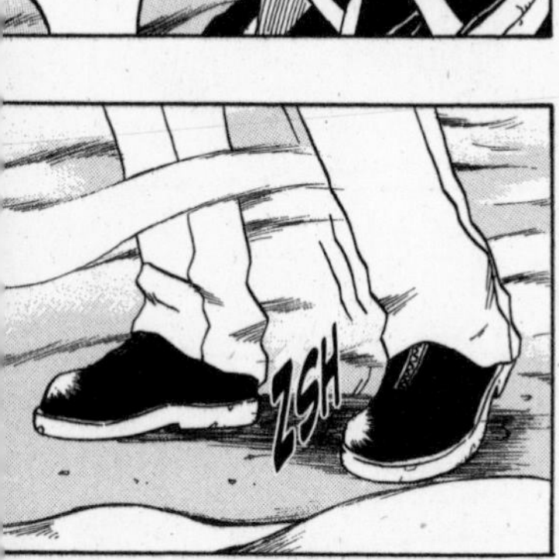
ZSH

WH... WHAT?! I'M...SH... SHAKING...

WH... WHO'S THERE? SHOW YOURSELF!!
CHANK

YOU...

KIRIN.
RIGHT.

THE ICY FEELING...
...STOPPED ...

HSSSH

TCH.

WHAT ARE YOU DOING HERE? DID YOU DO THIS?!
SWSH

HEY. LONG TIME NO SEE, WISE.
YOU CAN KEEP MEXIS IF YOU WANT. I JUST CAME TO TOWN TO COLLECT THIS.
AND I THOUGHT I'D JUST SHOW MY FACE BEFORE I LEFT.
CHAK
RBB RBB
HIS HEAD...
SO THAT OLD MAN WAS A CYBORG, HUH...

YOU DON'T ACTUALLY THINK YOU KNOW *EVERYTHING* ABOUT THE ZENOM SYNDICATE, RIGHT?
IT'S THE SAME WITH ME, TOO. IT'S ALL UNDER MASTER KUJAKU'S...
SP

VSH
LOOKS LIKE YOU'VE GOT COMPANY. SEE YOU LATER THEN.
BM
HSSSH
VSH
WHO IS IT?

WUB
WUB
URGH... I'VE GOT A SPLITTING HEADACHE. AAH...IT HURTS...
YOU!!
YOU'RE ALIVE... HOW DID YOU GET UP HERE? CAN IT BE–
HUH?
AND I THOUGHT I WAS JUST HAVING A WEIRD DREAM...
TP
TP
HEEEY, SO THIS IS WHERE YOU ARE!!
GOTCHA, YOU PHONY MAGICIAN!!
UUUURGH, YELLING HURTS TOO...
WUB
...THERE'S NOWHERE YOU CAN RUN TO, YOU BRAT.
MY GOAL IS WORLD DOMINATION. I'VE GOT NO INTENTION OF...
...RUNNING AWAY.
G G G G G
PHEW...
THIS TIME...

LET'S BEGIN THIS CARNIVAL OF BLOOD!

LOOKS LIKE I'VE GOT A FREE TICKET TO RIDE.

RELEASE SPIRIT!!!

FSH

DM
DM
DM
I'LL STRIKE FIRST!!!

BM

TP

TCH.

SHUP

SW

SH

ON THE WAY DOWN, I'LL GET HIM WITH A HEEL-DROP.

SP

VMP

GRRR

HAK

SP
FWA
GOTCHA!!!
WHSH
WHOA.

WHAP

URGH!!!

ZSH
ZSH
ZS!!

COME ON NOW, AREN'T YOU PLANNING ON TAKING OVER THIS WORLD?
SLLRP
SLLRP

YOU CAN'T EVEN LAY A FINGER ON ME...
FWA
FWA
TP

DAMN IT... I HAVEN'T BEEN ABLE TO HIT HIM EVEN ONCE...

IT'S SLOW... I CAN DODGE IT EASILY.

HE'S JUST CHARGING AT ME ON HIS O-PART.

A BRAT LIKE YOU, WHO CAN'T EVEN TELL WHICH WAY THE WIND BLOWS, SHOULDN'T EVEN DARE TO DREAM!!

NOW.

GN

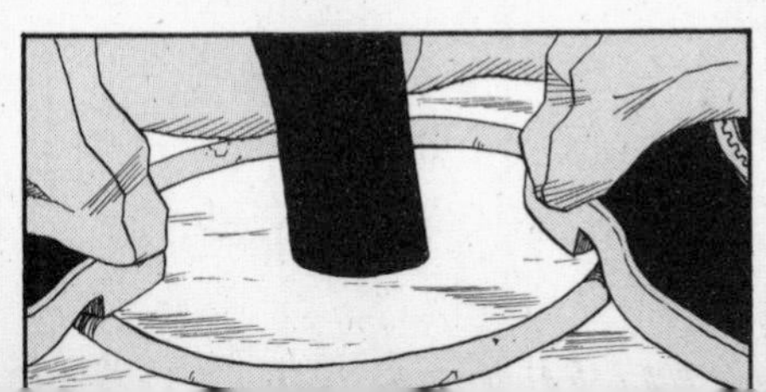

FLAP FLAP
WAA WAA
SSSSH
...IT'S US, THE ZENOM SYNDI-CATE!!!
CATCH!!
THUD
DM

SPNN

DM

ZP

HUUUUH? YOU COULDN'T DODGE IT... COULD YOU, LITTLE BOY?
USING YOUR O-PART MEANS USING *THIS* PART OF YOUR BODY— *THIS PART.*
TP TP

WHA... WHAT *WAS* THAT?

I KNEW IT...HE'S STRONG... BUT I ALREADY KNOW WHAT HIS O-PART'S EFFECT IS.
HE WON'T GET ME WITH THE SAME MOVE AGAIN...

I'VE ALREADY TOLD YOU THAT YOU'RE NOT GOING TO BE ABLE TO LAY A FINGER ON ME.
YOUR FATE WAS SEALED FROM THE MOMENT YOU DECIDED TO FIGHT.

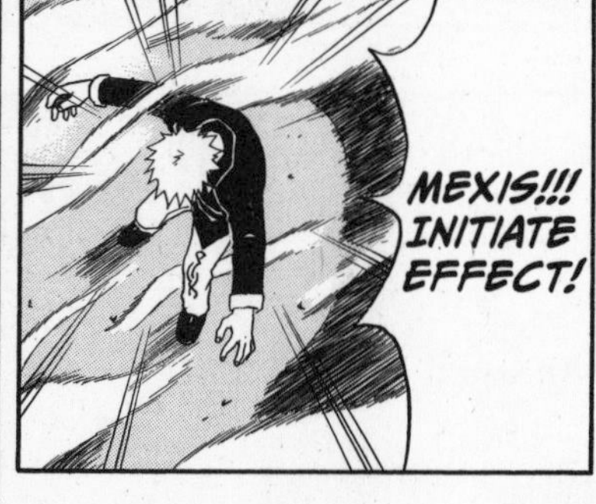
MEXIS!!! INITIATE EFFECT!

MEXIS?

ZM
ZM
ZM
IF YOU CAN'T EVEN DEFEAT ME, YOUR SILLY LITTLE DREAMS ARE FINISHED.
SLLRP SLLRP

BSSSSH
!!!
WHOA.
A L... LASER.

I'VE CONNECTED MY NERVE SYSTEMS WITH MEXIS, BUT IT DOESN'T HURT AS MUCH AS BEFORE.
LOOKS LIKE MOST OF THE BODY'S REGENER-ATED.
WAIT... THE LASER'S ...
!!
SWSSH
BM
TH... THIS IS...
SWSH

DMP
PLIP
PLIP
PLIP

NO! THE DENSE STEAM AROUND US SHOULD HAVE WEAKENED THE LASER!
STEAM IS BASICALLY LIKE CLOUDS, SO IF THERE'S A LOT OF IT...
...IT INTERFERES WITH THE SATELLITE TRANSMISSION, AND IT DOESN'T LET SUNLIGHT THROUGH.
HMM.
SO HE SHOULDN'T BE ABLE TO USE IT TO ATTACK ME...BUT IT'S SO POWERFUL...

DAMN IT, I HAVEN'T BEEN ABLE TO DO ANYTHING YET.

SLLLSH!

SLLLSH!!

SP

WHOA!!

MWA HA HA!

DAMN IT, IT'S ATTACKING ME FROM ALL DIRECTIONS...
IT'S TOO FAST!!! I CAN'T DODGE IT!!!
VSH

HUH?!
H

VSH
TCH.
ALL THE ATTACKS ARE...

!!
I...
...I GOT IT.

I'VE GOT IT AT LAST.
HUFF
HUFF

LOOKS LIKE YOU'VE FINALLY FIGURED IT OUT.
HUP

CSHHHH
I PLACED ONE OF MY O-PARTS IN FRONT OF WHERE THE LASER IS FIRED FROM...
FWA FWA

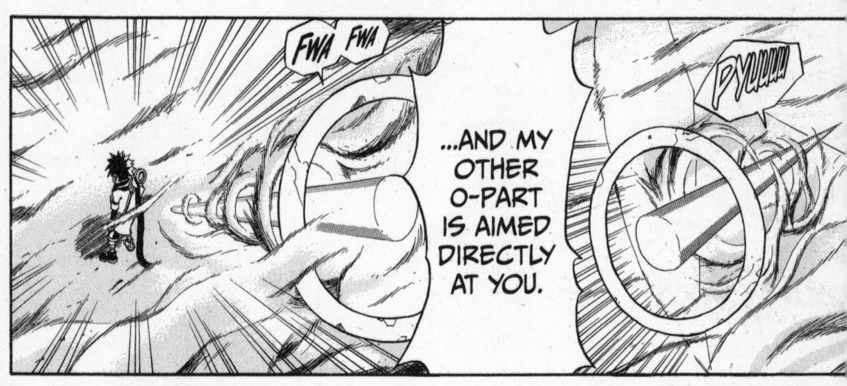
PYUUUU
...AND MY OTHER O-PART IS AIMED DIRECTLY AT YOU.
FWA FWA

URGH!!!
VSH
WHUP

SO IT'S AS IF THERE WERE NO STEAM AT ALL.
WZZZ
STEAM
PM

I REALLY GET TURNED ON AT THE SIGHT OF BLOOD. MWA HA HA... SO I'M GOING TO SMEAR YOUR RED BLOOD...
...ALL OVER THIS PLACE.

MWA HA HA HA. YOU'RE SHAKING.
BRR

LOOKS LIKE YOU FINALLY SEE WHO'S REALLY NUMBER ONE. SCARED... HUH?
I TOLD YOU BEFORE, DIDN'T I? IF YOU WANT TO LIVE, THEN JUST KEEP RUNNING AWAY FROM THOSE STRONGER THAN YOU.

AS LONG AS YOU KEEP YOUR HEAD DOWN AND OBEY THE COMMANDS OF THOSE ABOVE YOU, YOU'LL NEVER BE HURT. JUST LIKE THE PEOPLE OF THIS TOWN...
MWA HA HA

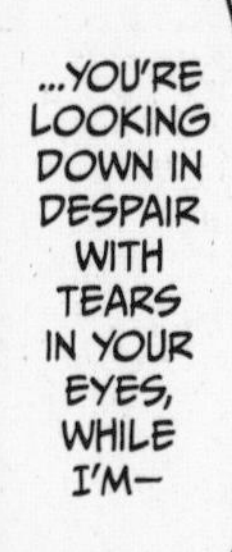
...YOU'RE LOOKING DOWN IN DESPAIR WITH TEARS IN YOUR EYES, WHILE I'M—

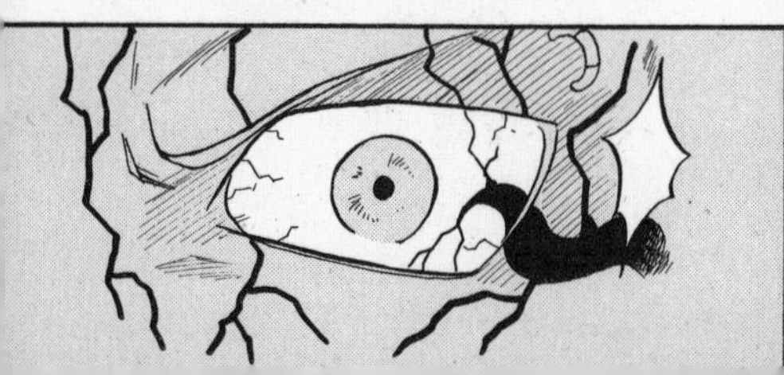

HEH

SORRY TO DISAPPOINT YOU, BUT MY EYES ARE TEAR-FREE.

HUP

DOOM

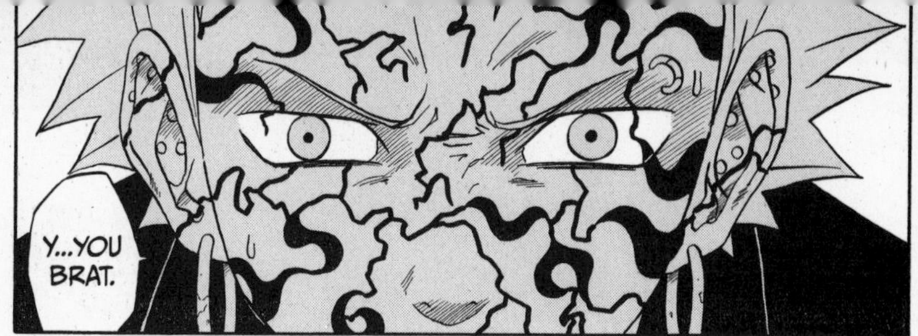
Y...YOU BRAT.

AND THE PEOPLE OF THIS TOWN ARE HOLDING THEIR HEADS HIGH NOW! GET IT?!!

I'M NOT GOING TO LET YOU DO ANYTHING TO THIS TOWN!!!
THIS TOWN'S GOING TO BE MINE!!!

...

BUT BEFORE THAT...

...I'M GOING TO BEAT THE LIVING DAY-LIGHTS OUT OF YOU!!!

HUH, YOU CAN ACT TOUGH, BUT IT'S NOT GOING TO MAKE ANY DIFFERENCE.
YOU'RE NOT GOING TO BE ABLE TO DODGE THE LASERS IF THEY ATTACK YOU FROM YOUR BLIND SPOTS.
KMM

I HAVE TO CALM DOWN AND REMEM-BER...
...THE TRAINING I HAD AT KIRIN'S PLACE ...

THE LASERS ARE ATTACKING ME FROM MY BLIND SPOTS...
MY BLIND SPOTS...
WHOOSH
FROM MY BLIND SPOTS... STONES...

THAT'S IT. STONES— THOSE STONES!!!
GO, BAT-MAN!!!

WHAT THE HELL ARE YOU TALKING ABOUT? GET READY, KID.

IMAGINE I'M IN THAT ROOM...

SHWOOOO
SHHHK
!!!
I GET IT!!!

SHWOOOO
OOPS.

THIS ISN'T A GAME, AND I DEFINITELY DON'T HAVE A BAT THIS TIME...
HSSSH
SHAKE
SHAKE
SPLURT
SHAKE
SHAKE
SHAKE
I SURE AM GLAD BALL ISN'T HERE...
TCH. YOU LUCKY LITTLE TURD.
SWISH

SWISH
SP
SWISH
OOH.
BM
WHOA.
BM
YEAH.
BM

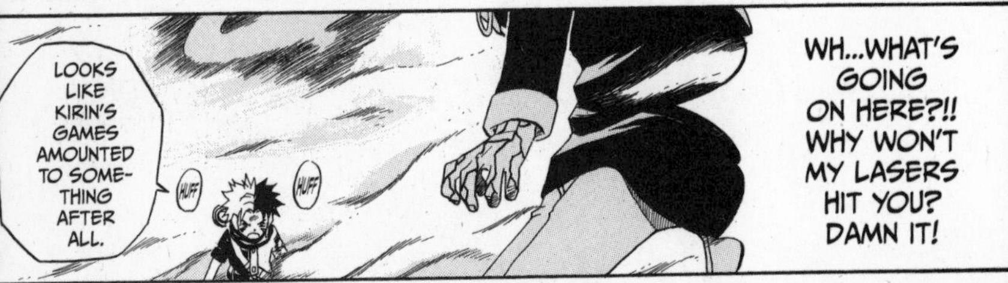

TCH... SO ATTACKING YOU FROM YOUR BLIND SPOTS IS USELESS, HUH?

SUU

SUU

YOU CERTAINLY HAVE CHANGED QUITE A BIT.

I MUSTN'T FORGET THIS FEELING... I'M NOT GOING TO BE ABLE TO DO MY BEST IF I PANIC.

THAT'S ONE THING I'VE LEARNED. YEAH.

BM

BM

THEN I'M GOING TO KILL YOU WITH MY *OWN* SPECIAL MOVE. TOYING AROUND WITH YOU HAS LOST ITS APPEAL.

THIS CARNIVAL IS...

...OVER.

GGGG

SPECIAL MOVE.

CRAK
SHWUP
CRAK
MAGIC MARION-ETTE.
SWSH
SWSH
DANGLE

WHOA, THAT'S NASTY ...
WARRRGH
SPNN
SNFF
SPNN
GRP
AAARGH!!!

HMMM
CRAK

DAN
GLE
FWA
FWA
URGH.

H...HE'S FLOATING. AND THAT BODY... THAT'S NO ORDINARY ATTACK.
IT'S LIKE A HUGE WHIP. I BLOCKED HIS ATTACK, BUT HE STILL GOT ME.
HUFF
HUFF

IF I TAKE A DIRECT HIT, IT MIGHT BE THE END OF ME.

I'M GOING TO MAKE A HUGE PIERCING OUT OF YOUR BELONGINGS AFTER YOU DIE.

DAMN IT.
CHAK

FWOOO
BWM
YEEARGH!!!
MMM

VWUP

MWA HA HA.

WFFF

NOW YOU'VE GOT NOTHING TO GUARD YOURSELF WITH. WHAT ARE YOU GOING TO DO?

GRP

DM

PUNCH YOU.

SNAP SNAP
!!!
THAT'S RIGHT, THE KID'S O-PART ...
...IS A BOOMER-ANG.
D... DAMN IT, HE'S CUT THROUGH THE WIRES.
SO THIS IS WHAT HE WAS AIMING FOR...
W...WAIT A MINUTE. I CAN'T PUT MY BODY TOGETHER THAT QUICKLY.
THINGS ARE NOT WHAT THEY SEEM TO BE.
YOU BETTER REMEMBER THAT.
AND NOW, AS I SAID BEFORE, I'M GOING TO...
GRSH
GRSH
GRP

...BEAT THE LIVING DAY-LIGHTS OUT OF YOU!!!

ZSH ZSH ZSH

YEEEEES! I FINALLY HIT HIM...!! OOOH, THAT FELT SOOO GOOD...!!!

RAAAA

GRRR. NOW I'M REALLY GONNA MAKE YOU SUFFER!!!

GW!!!
I NEVER THOUGHT I'D HAVE TO USE THIS MOVE...
...AGAINST A BRAT LIKE YOU.
GW!!!

マジックホール・ワールド
MAGIC HOLE WORLD

HIS O-PART'S GOTTEN WIDER.

I'M GOING TO TRANSPORT YOUR WHOLE BODY TO HELL.

GO!!
BM
KN
HUH, YOU'RE NOT GOING TO BE ABLE TO GET ME WITH A MOVE LIKE THAT!!
SP
TP
FWAI
BM
WHOA, THAT WAS CLOSE!!!

YIKES!!
RSH
SWAAAA
ZSH ZSH ZSH
GWSSH
ZP ZP ZP ZP
TMP
DAMN IT.
SPNN SPNN

HEH
YOU'VE JUMPED UP...

SHHP

!!

SHOOT!! I CAN'T CHANGE DIREC-TIONS IN MIDAIR.
SP

SHAKE SHAKE
SHAKE SHAKE
NUUUUU-UURGH...

CLANK
CLANK
WHOA.
ZWSH

POOF
WHERE AM I?!!

RIGHT ON THE TIP OF MEXIS'S HORN.
SLURP

GUUUUU-UURGH!

HEY, YOU FORGOT SOME-THING.

SHHHHP

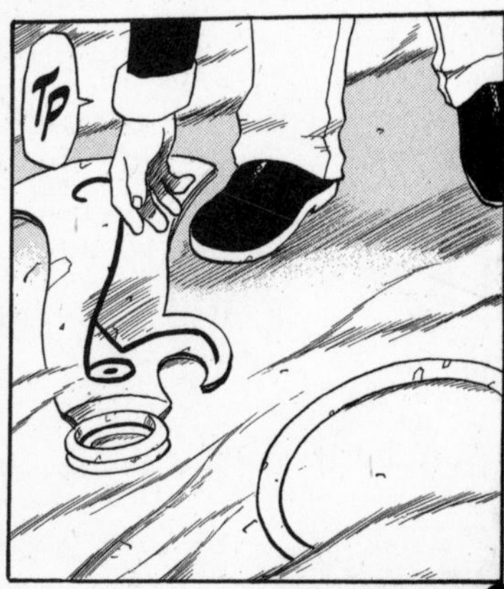

I... I...

...CAN'T MOVE...

YOU'RE GOING TO BE DYED CRIMSON WITH YOUR OWN O-PART! *MWA HA HA HA.*

RRRSSSSHH

CHAPTER 24: BLUE SKY

RRSSSH

YOU'RE SKEWERED LIKE A PIG AND NOW YOUR OWN O-PART IS GONNA DO YOU IN!

URGH... I CAN'T...
ZLSH

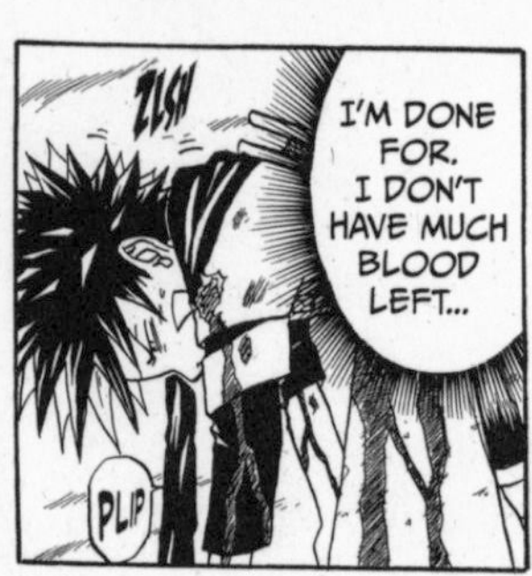
ZLSH
I'M DONE FOR. I DON'T HAVE MUCH BLOOD LEFT...
PLIP

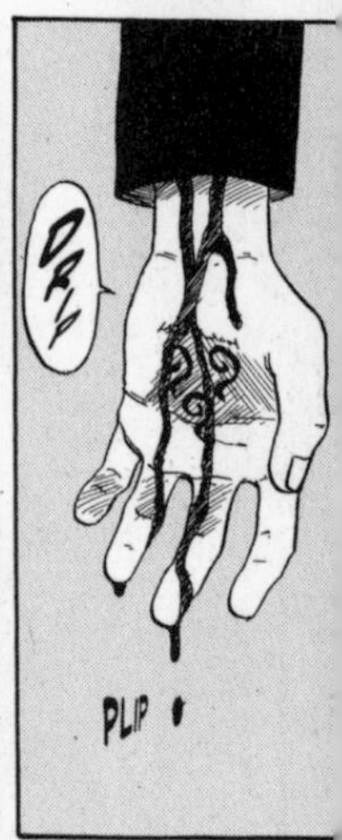
DRIP
PLIP

!!

SHVR
TH... THIS IS... THE NUMBER OF THE BEAST–666.
SHVR

I REMEMBER NOW!!
B...BUT WASN'T THAT A DREAM?

INITIATE EFFECT!!!
GWOOOO
AAAA-AAAH!
IT...IT'S SUCKING UP MY SPIRIT WITH INCREDI-BLE FORCE.
S... SOME-THING'S HAPPENING TO MY BODY...
THIS TOWN'S NOT GOING TO CHANGE.
YOU, AND ALL THE SCUM IN THIS TOWN, ARE GOING TO DIE WITH YOUR HEADS TURNED DOWN– JUST AS YOU'VE ALWAYS DONE.

WHAP

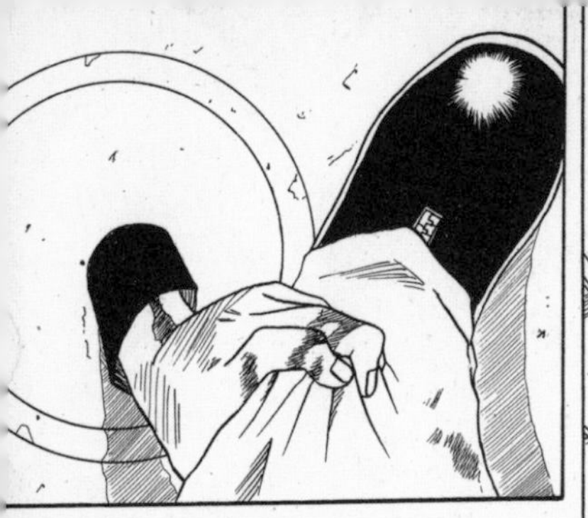

MWA HA... HA HA HA HA HA. I LIKE THAT. YOU'RE STRUGGLING IN VAIN. BUT MY O-PART, BROTHER, HAS ALREADY SHRUNK BACK.
YOU'RE NOT GOING TO BE ABLE TO GET YOUR BODY THROUGH !!

THAT'S NOT THE POINT. I NEEDED TO GRAB YOU...
...AND NOW MY LEFT HAND IS GOING TO ABSORB YOUR O-PART'S EFFECT.

S-K-WEEEZ
THIS ISN'T AN ORDINARY LEFT HAND. THIS IS THE POWER OF 666. YOU'RE...
SHUU

...GOING TO GET A TASTE OF YOUR OWN O-PART'S EFFECT!!
GRSH
HOW COME THAT BRAT CAN USE THE SAME TRANSPORTATION EFFECT AS MY O-PART...?!!
AAAAA-AAARGH!

FP
HUH?!!
HAKK
FP
URGH.
THUD
WHA ...!!
WHAT'S GOING ON?!!
ZLSH

THUD

DMP

THE SAME BLOOD FLOWS THROUGH ALL OF US. MAYBE NOW YOU UNDERSTAND THAT.

HUFF

HUFF

AAAA-AAARGH... BLOOD. RED BLOOD IS COMING OUT. NO, NO! MY BLOOD...

WOBBL

WOBBL

MY...MY HAND... N... NO WAY...

SHAKE

SHAKE

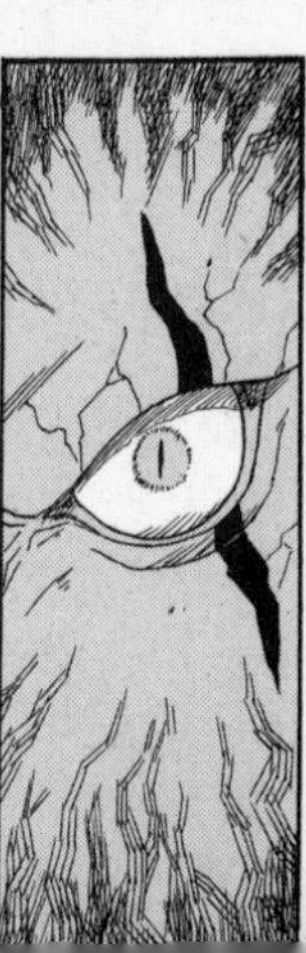

GWSH
SWSH

GWOOOOP
WHA... WHAT THE HELL IS THIS?!! MEXIS... STOP IT... YOU CAN'T EAT ME!!
LET GO OF ME, DAMN IT!!!

URGH ...
WH... WHAT'S GOING ON?
HUFF
HUFF

S... STOP... IT...

URGH ...
S... STOP... IT...

GYUUUU

ZWRRR

SOME-THING'S WRONG WITH THAT MONSTER.
JIO...

!!

WHOA.

D...DAMN IT... THIS MONSTER'S ABSORBED WISE'S SPIRIT OF HATRED ...
...AND IS BEGINNING TO GATHER STRENGTH WITHIN ITSELF. AT THIS RATE...

GYUUUUUU

THERE IT IS!!

GRP

BLLG

THUD

FWAAAA

HUH?

KIRIN, THIS DOESN'T LOOK VERY GOOD...
DAMN IT, WE'RE NOT GOING TO BE ABLE TO ESCAPE IN TIME.

BIG BROTHER! JIO!!!

THIS ISN'T GOOD.

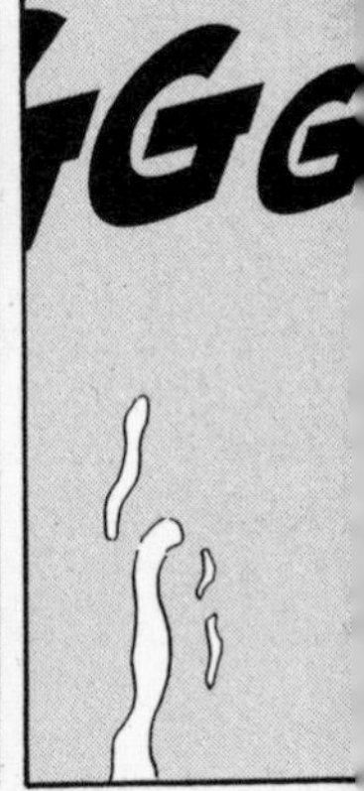

I DON'T HAVE TIME...
HUFF
HUFF
I'M...
...TO WASTE IN A PLACE LIKE THIS.
O.P.T.: JIO FREED
I'M...

...GOING TO TAKE OVER THIS WORLD!!!
D-PART: NEW ZERO-SHIKI
RANK: B
YEEEERGH!

EFFECT: TRIPLE
(INCREASING POWER BY
A FACTOR OF THREE)

BK
CRSH
WHOA!!!
OOF.

ENTOTSU-CITY
BOOOOSH
THD
ENTO

POK
POK

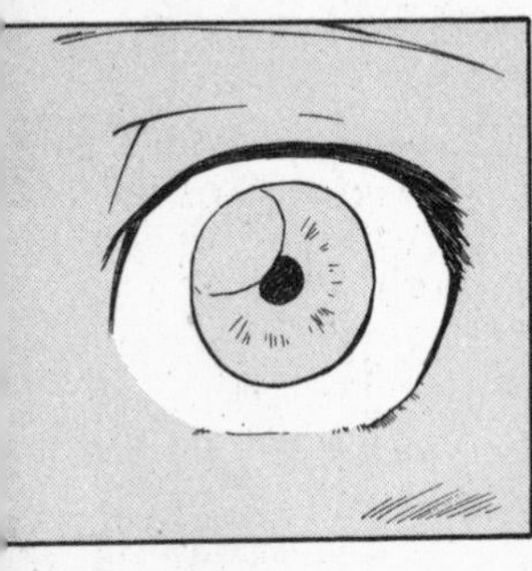

OWW.

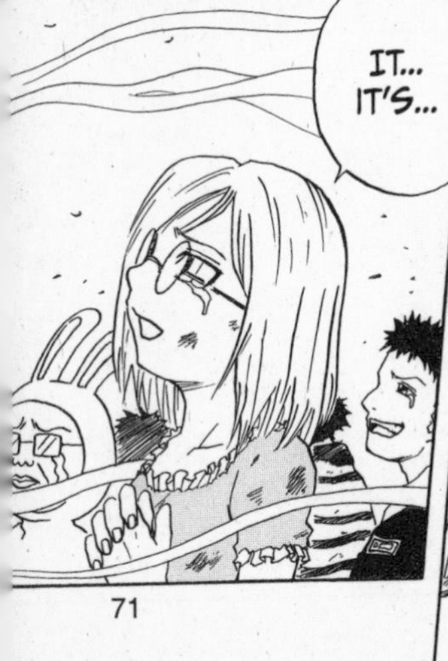
IT... IT'S...

THE MONSTER... STOPPED MOVING...

BWM
BWM

GSSH

THIS IS JIO'S... AND LOOK RIGHT THERE.
OH.
PWIK
PWIK

...

JIO...

WORLD DOMINATION, THAT'S MY DREAM.

JIO...

SO I'VE GOT TO FIGHT.
WITH MY HEAD HELD HIGH.

JIO...

I'M GOING TO BEAT THE LIVING DAYLIGHTS OUT OF THAT GUY.

THANK YOU...

YO, I KNEW IT. YOU REALLY *ARE* SOMETHING.
SNIFF
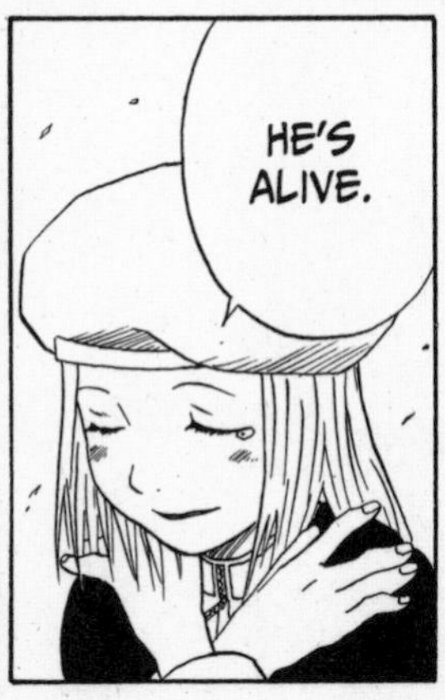
HE'S ALIVE.

Z-Z-Z
Z-Z-Z

MY HEART... ALL OF ME.
IT FEELS AS IF I COULD BE ABSORBED INTO THE SKY.
PLIP

IT'S BLUE...

WAAA
WAAA
MOTHER, HELP ME...
HANG IN THERE, JILL! I'LL SAVE YOU!

I'D COMPLETELY FORGOTTEN THIS FEELING...

I'LL GET YOU OUT OF THERE IN A MINUTE!!
JUST HANG IN THERE.
DSSH

ZCH

YOU!! WHAT ARE YOU DOING?!!

TH... THANKS, MISTER.

NO, WE'RE THE ONES WHO SHOULD THANK YOU.

HUP

THE MONSTER STOPPED MOVING.

THE WALLS AROUND THE TOWN HAVE FALLEN DOWN!

WE'VE WON.

WE'RE FREE...

WE GOT OUR BLUE SKY BACK!!!

WAAAAAAAAA

THE DAY OF DEPARTURE

YOU'RE LEAVING ALREADY...? ARE YOU SURE YOU'RE OKAY?!

YEAH

WOW

YEAH, I'M FINE. I'M FINE.

YO, YOU DON'T LOOK FINE TO ME.
HUH?! SHUT UP!!!

SP

THIS FREEDOM'S BEEN BUILT UPON THE SACRIFICES OF MANY PEOPLE.
TO MAKE SURE THAT THAT DOESN'T GO TO WASTE, WE'RE ALL GOING TO RAISE OUR HEADS UP HIGH...
...AND DO OUR BEST.

BUT THE ONE WHO LIFTED THE MIST THAT WAS HANG-ING OVER OUR MINDS...
...WAS YOU, JIO.

THANKS.
I THANK YOU ON BEHALF OF THE RESISTANCE MOVEMENT AND ALL THE PEOPLE OF THIS TOWN.

OH, I WAS ONLY DOING MY JOB AS A BODYGUARD, PROTECTING RUBY.
IT JUST GOT ON MY NERVES THAT WISE AND THE ZENOM SYNDICATE KEPT GETTING IN MY WAY.
AND THAT MONSTER WOULD HAVE GOTTEN IN MY WAY OF WORLD DOMINATION, TOO.
SHAKE
SHAKE

I GUESS THIS TOWN'S MY FIRST STEP TOWARDS WORLD DOMINATION. HA HA HA.
SO YOU WEREN'T FIGHTING FOR US AFTER ALL...
Ugh~
I KNEW IT. HE'S...

FOR REAL
WHY WOULD I GO AND DO SOMETHING LIKE THAT?

YOU IDIOT!! THAT WAS UNCALLED FOR!!!
JUST KEEP YOUR USUAL WORKER-FOR-HIRE ATTITUDE AND YOU'LL BE A HERO!
DING
OH!!!

I...I WAS ONLY JOKING... I'M ACTUALLY A WORKER-FOR-HIRE.
MY FEE IS...
WAA
MONEY ?!!

WHAK
YOU'RE ONLY MAKING THINGS WORSE, SO STOP TALKING!
OUCH !!!

HA HA HA

HA HA HA

BY THE WAY, DID YOU FEEL A STRANGE CHILL BACK THEN?
YEAH, I DID. JUST WHEN I SAW THAT THING THAT LOOKED LIKE A DEMON FLYING AROUND.
DID YOU SEE IT? IT PROBABLY CAME OUT OF THAT MONSTER.

URK

GRP

I...
I KNEW IT.

THAT WASN'T A DREAM AFTER ALL.
WAS THAT ME...? ANOTHER ME... INSIDE ME?
AM I THE ONE WHO'S BEEN MAKING EVERYBODY UNHAPPY ALL THIS TIME?

JIO...

YOU'RE YOU, JIO.

SLAP
SLAP
NOW, NOW, WHAT'S THERE TO GET BLUE ABOUT?!
HUH?
YOU'RE A GUY WHO'S GOING FOR WORLD DOMINATION!!!

WU... WUBY...

THAT'S RIGHT, I'M JIO FREED! THE GUY WHO'S GOING TO TAKE OVER THIS WORLD!!!
HAA HA HA
DOOM
GOOD!!

WHAT...? YOU'RE REALLY GOING TO LEAVE US, BIG BROTHER ?!!
SERIOUSLY, BALL?
AWW
YEAH.
NOOO

HE'S REALLY GOING TO LEAVE US...
SPHERE ...

I WANT TO BECOME STRONGER ...
KRP
ZWSH
AND I WANT TO HELP PEOPLE WHO ARE IN THE KIND OF TROUBLE WE'VE BEEN THROUGH!!

YO, AFTER ALL, I AM AN O.P.T.
THAT WAS SO COOL...
DOON

BIG BROTHER...

WE'RE GONNA MISS YOU.
WAA-ARGH...
GOOD LUCK, BALL.
THIS... IS SO TOUCHING...
BALL, YOU...!!

WAIT... YOU'RE COMING WITH US?
IS HE AN O.P.T. ?!!
DON'T SPOIL THIS TENDER MOMENT, DAMN IT!!!

BALL, THERE'S ONE LAST THING I HAVE TO SAY TO YOU.

GRP

DAD...

YOU'RE A BIG BOY NOW—YOU'RE TOO OLD TO BE PLAYING O.P.T.S.

DAD.

AND I BET YOU'VE GOT A CRUSH ON THAT RUBY GIRL. THAT'S WHY YOU'RE ACTUALLY GOING...

DAD.

N... NO WAY. YO, YOU'VE GOT IT WRONG...
HA... HA HA
HMMM...
I...I'M SO JEALOUS OF HIM...
HE SAW STRAIGHT THROUGH ME...

SEE YA.
GOOD LUCK, BIG BROTHER.
OKAY!
...

...

NICE, ISN'T IT?
UH-HUH.

I WONDER IF I'VE GOT A FATHER AND MOTHER SOME-WHERE ...
WHAT DO THEY LOOK LIKE? MAYBE THEY LOOK LIKE ME.

FWSH
FWSH

I NEVER KNEW JIO COULD LOOK LIKE THIS.

K.L.

THEY'RE REALLY GOING.
SP

SO I'VE GOT TO FIGHT WITH MY HEAD HELD HIGH.
MY DREAM IS...
CHIRP

IF THIS IS YOUR WAY OF TAKING OVER THE WORLD... THEN...
...I'M ALL FOR IT, KID.
...WORLD DOMINATION!!!
FLAP

WHOA, THAT WAS CLOSE.
THE RUBBLE FROM THAT HUGE CHIMNEY HAS SPREAD REALLY FAR...
...SO YOU SHOULD BE CAREFUL WHERE YOU WALK.

YO, YO, SO WHERE WE HEADED TO, HUH?
THIS JOURNEY'S GOING TO BE SO EXCITING!! YEAH!
...
HEY! GET YOUR FOOT OFF MY SCARF.

WELL, I'M YOUR TYPICAL, RUN-OF-THE-MILL TREASURE HUNTER...
...SO I GUESS WE'RE GOING TO HEAD TO SOME RUIN AND LOOK FOR O-PARTS.
I'VE GOT THE GPS I BOUGHT AT ENTOTSU CITY, SO FROM NOW ON...
...IT'S GOING TO BE EASIER TO LOCATE PLACES THAN JUST LOOKING AT A MAP.
YOU CAN USE THAT NOW?! LET ME SEE.
HEY!

AAAH...
SO YOU COLLECT O-PARTS, HUH, RUBY?
KIRIN'S GOT LOADS OF THEM AT HIS PLACE.

RIGHT, JIO?
HUH...? DID HE?
WOW... I CAN PINPOINT EXACTLY WHERE WE ARE.
BIP
WHAT?! REALLY?

COME TO THINK OF IT...
...KIRIN DIDN'T COME TO SEE US OFF.

OF COURSE HE DIDN'T. THE PEOPLE OF THIS TOWN DON'T LIKE HIM.
OH, RIGHT.

THEN OFF TO KIRIN'S HOUSE WE GO.

WE MADE SUCH A BIG EXIT FROM TOWN...
...AND NOW WE'RE GOING BACK? THAT SUCKS.

IT LOOKS LIKE YOU GUYS DON'T HAVE TIME FOR THAT.
HEY, IT'S—
KIRIN !!!

YOU THREE MIGHT HAVE CAUGHT THE ATTENTION OF BOTH THE GOVERNMENT AND THE SYNDICATE WITH THIS INCIDENT...
CRCH
SKWEEK
ESPECIALLY YOU, JIO.

...

TP
TP
AMIDABA'S GOT SOME-THING TO DO, SO SHE COULDN'T COME TO SEE YOU OFF.
RUBY... I DON'T KNOW WHAT AMIDABA TOLD YOU, BUT...

...SHE TOLD *ME* TO TELL *YOU* TO MEET A MAN NAMED WICK AT THE DASTOM RUINS...
DASTOM RUINS?
WICK?

DOES HE HAVE SOME-THING TO DO WITH MY FATHER?!

I DON'T KNOW...

OH, AND I'VE GOT ANOTHER MESSAGE FOR YOU GUYS...

POP

SHE SAID... TAKE CARE.
NOW, LET'S MAKE A TOAST TO YOUR JOURNEY, AND HERE'S A LITTLE SOUVENIR...
...A PICKLE.
酒

*SAKE

UGH

WAS IT REALLY OKAY TO LEAVE HIM THERE LIKE THAT?

AND WE CAN'T DRINK ALCOHOL EITHER.

I'VE HAD ENOUGH PICKLES FOR NOW.

TMP
TMP

OOOH...
WELL, SEE YA.

H...HEY, BALL...
...ARE YOU SAD TO PART WITH YOUR FAMILY...?
HUH?

YO, OF COURSE I AM. WHAT ARE YOU TALKING ABOUT? BUT THE ADVENTURE IS WHAT'S IMPORTANT NOW.

HEY, WHAT ARE *YOUR* PARENTS LIKE, JIO?
DO THEY HAVE BLACK AND WHITE HAIR LIKE YOU?

YOU STUPID DREAD-LOCK-HEAD! HOW COULD YOU?!

PAP

JIO!! YOU'RE ALREADY A MEMBER OF THE KID'S GANG OF THE RESISTANCE MOVEMENT.
SO ON BEHALF OF THE GANG...

...

...WE FEEL REALLY BAD ABOUT YOUR MOM AND DAD, BUT...

?!

YOU'RE NOW...

...A MEMBER OF OUR FAMILY.

TRIP

SPLAT
BING
CLANG
BANG

WH...WHAT ARE YOU DOING?

OUCH! I TRIPPED...
OH, MAN, I'M CRYING.
WUB
WUB
CLAK

HA... JIO'S TRYING TO HIDE HIS TEARS. THAT'S SO LIKE HIM.

YO, YOU'RE THE ONE WHO TOLD ME TO BE CAREFUL, YOU KNOW...
FOR GOD'S SAKE...

FLAP
DADDY ...
HERE.

OUR MINDS ARE AS CLEAR AS THE BLUE SKY ABOVE...
FWA
FWA
HEY, LOOK.
HUH?
...AND IF WE LOOK UP...
...WE CAN SEE THE BIRDS FLYING...
...FREELY AND STRONGLY.

O-Parts Hunter

Special! In the Workplace True Story

Art by Chiharu (assistant)!

Characters

MR. KISHIMOTO, OUR RESPECTABLE BOSS

TYPO

We had the strangest encounter the first time we met each other, but I've been enjoying my work with him and I'm doing my meager best to assist him.
I hope that O-Parts Hunter will get even more exciting than it is now, and I hope to improve my skills through Mr. Kishimoto's teachings.
Y. IWAMOTO.

THE ASCALD CONTINENT "BEANS DISTRICT": AN AREA FRAUGHT WITH CHAOS, THANKS TO RECKLESS O.P.T.S AND THEIR POWERS.

DOOOSH

DOOOSH

O-PARTS HUNTER EXTRA STORY:

JUSTICE

ZLLSH

BWOOOSH

O-PART TERRORISM IN THE FIRST DEGREE. SUSPECT GROUP: THE UBO CLAN.
ZM
WHAT'S THE MATTER?
ARE THE STEA GOVERNMENT'S SPECIAL FORCES NOTHING MORE THAN MASTERS OF RUNNING AWAY? WELL?

A MORNING STAR O-PART WITH AN EXPLOSION EFFECT.
KRCH
ZP

I'VE SURMISED MOST OF YOUR MOVES AND CAPABILITIES BY NOW.

I'M GOING TO ARREST ALL OF YOU AND CONFIS-CATE YOUR O-PARTS.
SP
BE PREPARED TO MEET DIVINE JUDGMENT. TIME TO SAY YOUR PRAYERS.
SHA
SHA
AREN'T YOU THE ONE WHO SHOULD BE PRAYING?

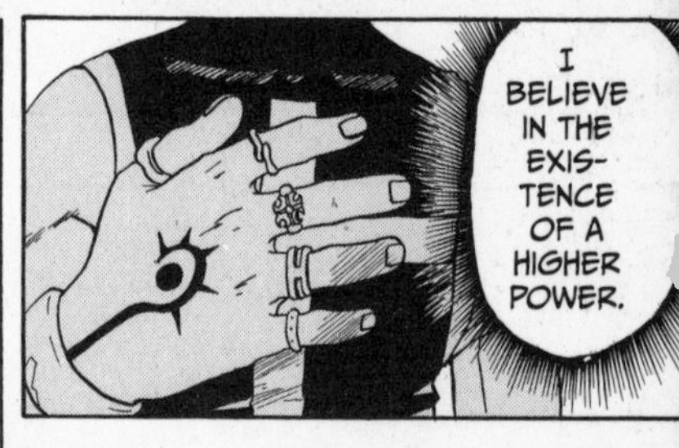
I BELIEVE IN THE EXIS-TENCE OF A HIGHER POWER.

YOU'RE NOT TELLING ME THAT THOSE RINGS ARE YOUR O-PARTS, ARE YOU?
HA HA HA, YOU'VE GOT TO BE KIDDING!!
HAHAHAHA
HA
HA
OR, TO BE MORE SPECIFIC...

HUH ?

—O-Parts Hunter Extra Story—

JUSTICE

RAIN...

AND I HATE THE SELFISH LOGIC OF GROWN-UPS...
MY PARENTS ABANDONED MY SISTER AND I...

I HATE RAIN...

...ON A RAINY DAY LIKE THIS...
WERE YOU ABLE TO SAY YOUR PRAYERS, LILY?
UH-HUH.
I PRAYED FOR MOMMY AND DADDY TO COME BACK AGAIN TODAY.
I'LL BRING YOU AN UMBRELLA.

IT'S BEGUN TO RAIN, BUT WE DIDN'T BRING AN UMBRELLA.
LOOKS LIKE IT'S NOT GOING TO STOP FOR A WHILE.
I'LL BRING AN UMBRELLA ...

LET'S RUN BACK BEFORE IT STARTS TO POUR.
WE'RE GOING TO GET WET ANYWAY.
THEN...

...I'LL RACE YOU BACK HOME, LILY!!
SEE YA.
HEY!!! THAT'S NOT FAIR, BIG BROTHER!!

I DON'T KNOW WHAT THEIR REASONS WERE...
...BUT I COULDN'T FORGIVE MY PARENTS FOR ABANDONING LILY, WHO WAS SUCH A INNOCENT CHILD.

OH NO!!

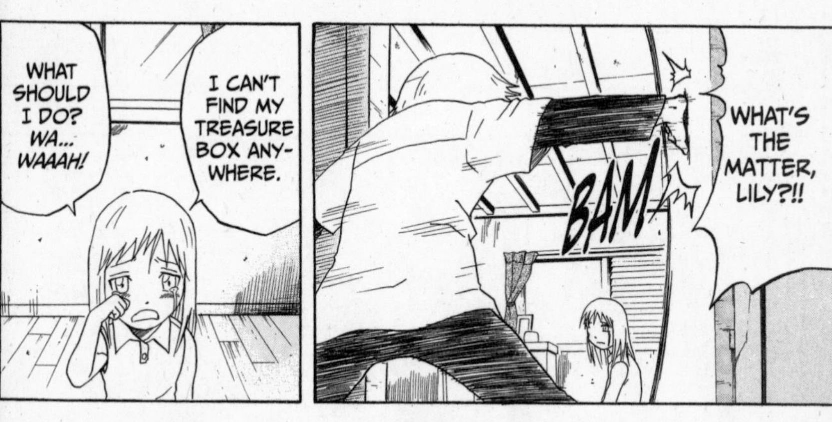

BAM
WHAT'S THE MATTER, LILY?!!
I CAN'T FIND MY TREASURE BOX ANY-WHERE.
WHAT SHOULD I DO? WA... WAAAH!

OH... REMEM-BER?
YOU LEFT THAT OUT ON THE TABLE DOWNSTAIRS BEFORE WE LEFT.
HA.

WHOA.
DM
THAT'S RIGHT!!

GULP
POK

WHAT DID I TELL YOU?
NOTHING'S MISSING. ♡

I'M SO GLAD.
OUR HOUSE SEEMED TOO LARGE FOR JUST THE TWO OF US TO BE LIVING IN IT.

CLAK
WELL, THEN...
...I'M OFF TO BUY SOME FOOD.
I'M COMING TOO.
NO!!! YOU HAVE TO STAY HOME, LILY.
WHAAAT? I ALWAYS HAVE TO STAY HOME. IT'S SO BORING.

OKAY, I'LL STAY HOME.
SEE YOU LATER.

THEN I'M NOT GOING TO LET YOU HAVE DINNER.
IS THAT WHAT YOU WANT?

SLAM

WHY WON'T HE EVER TAKE ME WITH HIM?
I DON'T LIKE BEING LEFT ALONE.

BIG BROTHER ...
ARE YOU...
DM
THIS IS ALL THAT'S LEFT...
...OF THE MONEY THE GOOD FATHER GAVE ME...
OH WELL.
GRP

WOOF
WOOF
EXCUSE ME.

WHAT?
GRRRR...
WOOF
COULD YOU SPARE SOME VEGETABLES AND BREAD? JUST A LITTLE WOULD BE FINE.

ARE YOU KIDDING? I'VE ALREADY LENT MONEY TO YOUR PARENTS!!
AND NOW THEIR BRAT'S ASKING FOR MORE! YOU SURE HAVE A LOT OF NERVE, KID!!

GO HOME!!!
SLAM

DAMN, WHAT DID WE EVER DO TO YOU?
I KNEW IT— I GUESS I'VE GOT NO OTHER CHOICE BUT TO ASK THE FATHER.

FLUTTER
FLUTTER

PLIP

UGH, I'M BORED.
LICK
HMM.
LICK
LICK

SLLRP
SLLRP
HEY, YOU. WHAT DO YOU THINK YOU'RE LOOKING AT?

HEY, IT'S THE GIRL WHO GOES TO CHURCH EVERY DAY.
AH, I'VE HEARD ABOUT HER.

MY MOM SAID HER PARENTS ABAN-DONED HER.
SHE'S TOO POOR TO HAVE A DECENT MEAL. THAT'S WHY SHE WAS STARING AT OUR POPSICLES.

YOU'RE WRONG! MOMMY AND DADDY ARE ON A VACA-TION...
...AND THEY'RE GOING TO COME BACK SOON!

HA HA HA. IT'S BEEN YEARS NOW. HOW CAN YOU STILL BELIEVE THAT?
IDIOT, YOUR PARENTS ABAN-DON—
SHUT UP!!!

...SHUT UP.

HEY, IT'S HER BROTHER.

LILY, I THOUGHT I TOLD YOU TO STAY HOME.
...

DAMN IT... RUN!!
DMP

I'M NOT HUNGRY AT ALL TODAY.

SO I DON'T MIND IF I DON'T EAT DINNER. REALLY.

LILY.

HUFF
HUFF

HA HA! THE GOOD FATHER GAVE ME SOME OF THE CHURCH'S COLLECTION MONEY, SO I'LL BE ABLE TO GET SOMETHING FOR LILY TODAY.
I CAN'T WASTE IT, BUT IT WOULDN'T HURT TO BUY HER A SWEET OR TWO.

HUFF
HUFF

WAIT UP, LILY.

I'M HOME.

LILY, I'VE GOT A LITTLE SURPRISE FOR YOU...
HUFF
HUFF
WELCOME HOME.

HUFF

WH... WHERE DID YOU GET THOSE, LILY?

TH... THE LADY NEXT DOOR ...
SP
...GAVE IT TO ME.

WHY ARE YOUR CLOTHES DIRTY?
AND WHY ARE YOU HIDING YOUR ARMS?
B-BMP

GRP
SHOW ME.
OH!
IT'S A WOUND.
A BITE MARK...

WHAT?! YOU'RE SO MEAN, BIG BROTHER!!!

I JUST...

...I'M JUST A NUISANCE TO YOU ALL THE TIME...

YOU'LL PROBABLY ABANDON ...

NEVER.

I'LL BECOME STRONG AND MAKE LOTS OF MONEY.

I'LL BUY YOU ANYTHING YOU WANT, LILY.

I'LL PROTECT YOU FOREVER... SO...

...SO PLEASE DON'T DO ANYTHING LIKE THIS AGAIN.

THANK YOU...

...BIG BROTHER.

TP
I KNOW.

WH... WHAT?

POK
RSTL
RSTL

AS LONG AS YOU'RE WITH ME, I DON'T NEED ANYTHING ELSE.
SO HERE'S A LITTLE PEACE OFFERING.
TH...THIS IS YOUR TREASURE, LILY... ARE YOU SURE?

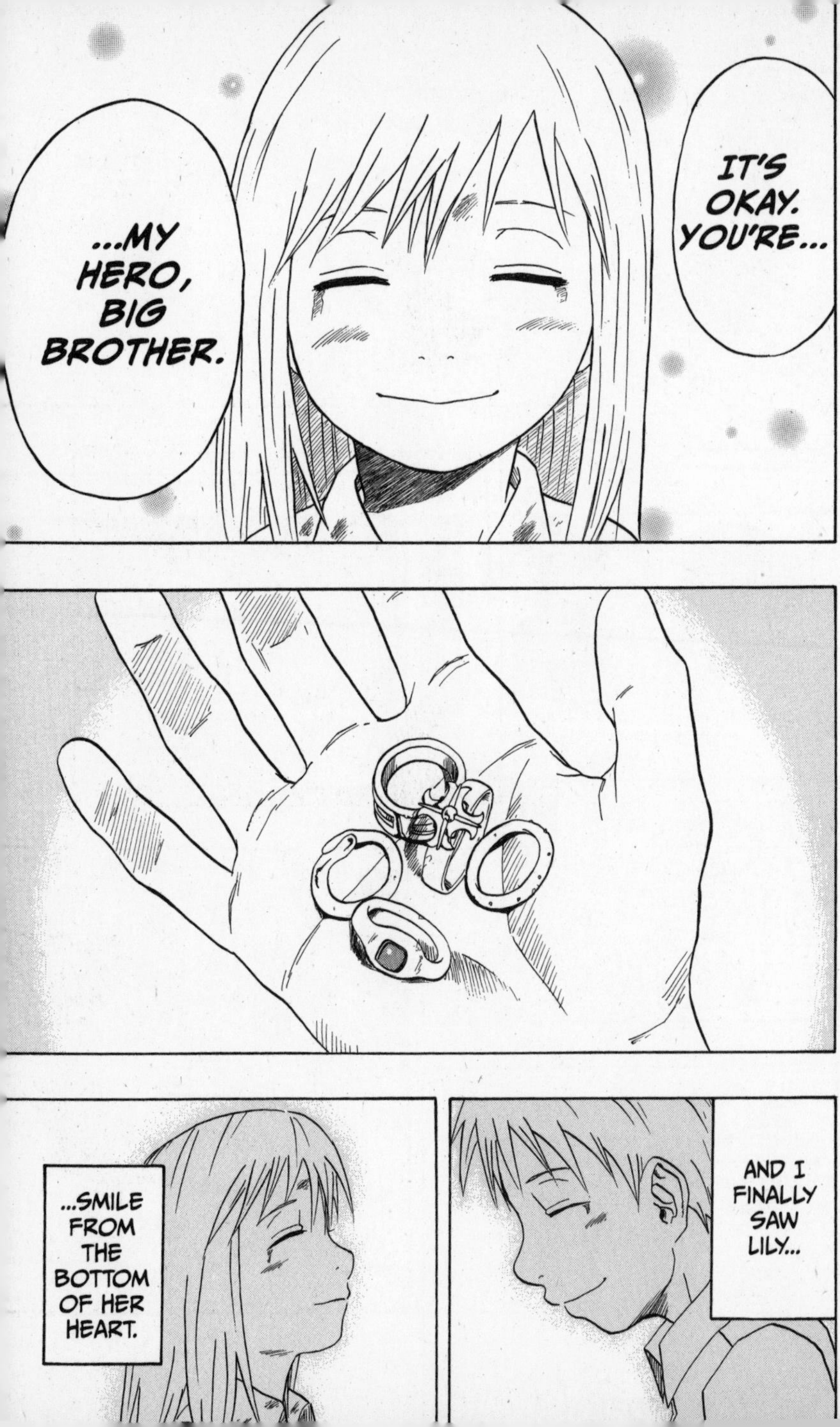

IT'S OKAY. YOU'RE...

...MY HERO, BIG BROTHER.

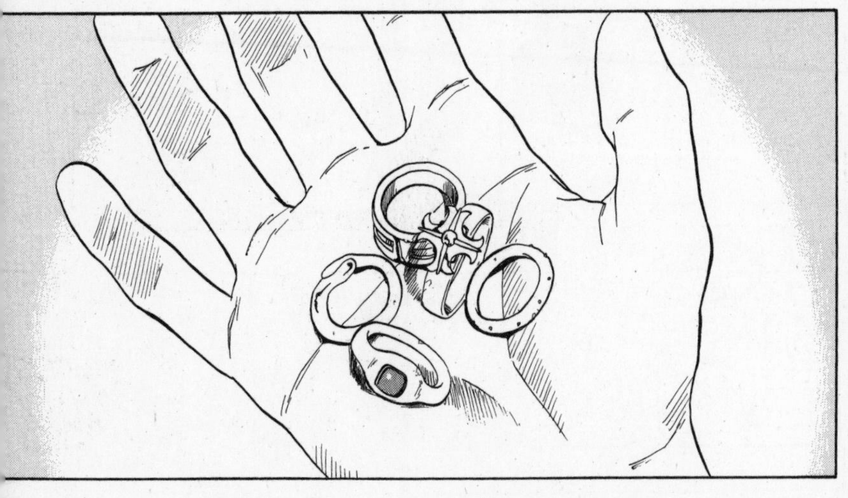

CHIRP
CHIRP

HUH.
RSH

HUP
WHOA!!!
ACK

O...OH, IT'S JUST SOME GUY...
I'VE NEVER SEEN ANYBODY IN THIS CHURCH EARLIER THAN US BEFORE.
PHEW.

OH!

AH, HE'S A KID.

OH, I'M SORRY. I TOOK THE LIBERTY...

...OF SPENDING THE NIGHT HERE.

OH NO, WE DON'T HAVE ANYTHING TO DO WITH THIS CHURCH.
BUT YOU SHOULD GO HOME QUICKLY. I'M SURE YOUR PARENTS ARE WORRIED ABOUT YOU.
I DON'T HAVE ANY PARENTS...
OH.

I'M FINE BEING ALONE. I'M NOT LONELY AT ALL.
I'VE GOT A DREAM NOW.
THAT'S WHY I'M TRAVELING AROUND.
I'M GOING TO BECOME STRONG AND FUL-FILL THAT DREAM.

THEN YOU'RE ...

SO HE'S THE SAME AS US...

I'M GOING TO BECOME AS STRONG AS ANY ADULT TOO.

BAAAM

WE'VE ONLY GOT EACH OTHER, SO I'M GOING TO PROTECT MY SISTER ALL THE TIME!!

YOU'RE EMBARRASSING ME, BIG BROTHER.

THEN YOU TWO ARE...

SP

I BET WE'LL GET ALONG.

WE'LL PROBABLY BE ABLE TO BECOME GOOD FRIENDS.
B-BMP
I...I SHOULD GET GOING.
SP
OH, YOU'RE GOING ALREADY?
WELL THEN, HERE'S TO BOTH OF US GETTING STRONGER IN THE FUTURE.
I HOPE WE'LL MEET AGAIN SOME-DAY.
UH... UH-HUH.
THANKS.

PHEW...

IT'S A NICE DAY TODAY.

FLAP

I'VE FOUND IT.
SUUU

SHUU
SHHH

LILY, I'M GOING AHEAD OF YOU.
TP TP
OOOH... WHAT A PRETTY FLOWER.

OH WELL.
WAIT FOR ME, BIG BROTHER.
I'M GOING TO LEAVE YOU IF YOU DON'T HURRY UP!

UH-HUH.
THANKS.
COME TO THINK OF IT, I TOLD HIM WE'D MEET EACH OTHER AGAIN SOMEDAY...
...BUT I FORGOT TO ASK... HIS NAME ...

I'LL REPLANT IT BACK HOME.

BIG BROTHER, LOOK!

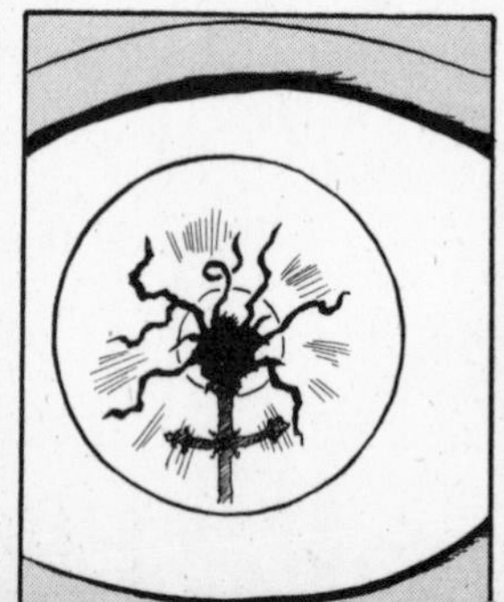

I'VE FOUND IT.
THE GREATEST DIAMOND IN THE ROUGH...
LONELINESS, HATRED, VENGEANCE...
I'M GOING TO PLANT THEM WITHIN YOU.
YOU'RE...
...ALL ALONE.

LILY!!!
WAAAAH
HUFF
HUFF
WH... WHERE ...
...AM I?
STEA GOVERNMENT HEADQUARTERS

WHAT DO YOU THINK ABOUT THAT BOY, AMIDABA?
WELL...
I DON'T THINK HE'S THE ONE.

EVERYTHING WITHIN A 50 KILOMETER RADIUS DISAPPEARED. MOUNTAINS, RIVERS, LAKES, EVERYTHING...

AND HE WAS THE ONLY ONE ALIVE IN THE MIDDLE OF THAT HUGE CRATER...
AND, ON TOP THAT, HE DIDN'T HAVE A SINGLE SCRATCH ON HIM.

IT MUST'VE BEEN CAUSED BY AN O-PART WITH AN EXPLOSION EFFECT.
I'M GUES-SING ITS RANK IS SOME-WHERE BETWEEN A HIGH "A" AND AN "S"...

HEY, KIRIN...
...YOU TOOK A LOOK AT THOSE O-PARTS THAT BOY HAD WITH HIM, RIGHT?

YEAH, THOSE ACTUALLY WERE O-PART RINGS, BUT THEIR RANK WAS A LOW "C."
THEY'VE DON'T HAVE AN EXPLOSION EFFECT, AND YOU'LL NEVER BE ABLE TO CREATE A CRATER THAT GIGANTIC WITH JUST THEM.

THE SS-RANKED O-PART BATTLESHIP SHIN IS GOING TO BE INSTALLED IN THE ATTACK FORCE.

AND ONLY THE BEST CAN GET ON BOARD.

I'M AS GOOD AS CHOSEN FOR THE SHIP...

HA HA HA.

AND I'LL BE PROMOTED TO SHIN'S COMMANDER-IN-CHIEF REAL SOON.

IN NO TIME I'LL HAVE YOU ALL IN THE PALM OF MY HAND. HA HA!

LOOKING FORWARD TO IT. HA HA HA HA.
KLAK KLAK
KEEP TALKING LIKE THAT AND SOME-ONE'S GONNA BREAK YOUR HAND...

隔離室
Isolation Room
LOCK

LILY.
A DREAM ...
IT'S GOT TO BE A DREAM... IT...MUST'VE JUST BEEN A NIGHT-MARE.

VSSSSH
TP
YOU WERE ASLEEP FOR A LONG TIME. HOW DO YOU FEEL?

WHERE'S MY SISTER LILY?!
SHE SHOULD HAVE BEEN WITH ME!!!
CALM DOWN...
I'M REALLY SORRY, BUT THERE WASN'T ANYBODY AROUND, APART FROM... WELL, WE DID FIND A FLOWER, BUT...

ACTUALLY, YOU'RE LUCKY TO BE ALIVE.
HUH?!
IT'S A MIRACLE ...
...TO HAVE SURVIVED THAT EXPLO- SION...

YOU'RE...
...ALL ALONE.
WUB
URGH.
HM.
666 ...?
666...
THAT'S THE NUMBER OF THE BEAST.
YOU HEAR ABOUT IT IN REFERENCE TO A MONSTER CALLED SATAN, BUT WHAT OF IT?

666

...

GRP
TMP
LILY.

LILY...
LILY CAN'T BE DEAD...
PSHHT
DM
HEY, YOU!! YOU MUST STAY HERE!!

WHAT'S THE MATTER?
SHHHP
THAT'S THE BOY FROM THE CRATER. HE'S ESCAPED— YOU'VE GOT TO CATCH HIM FOR ME.

SURE, I'LL CATCH HIM.
BUT I CAN'T ASSURE YOU THAT HE'LL BE UNHARMED.

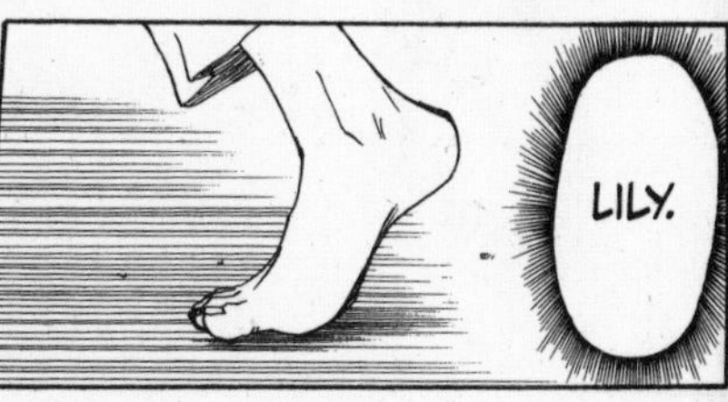
LILY.

HUFF
HUFF

SHP
SP
NO MORE PLAYING TAG, KID.

YOU'RE THE ONLY SURVIVOR OF THAT EXPLO- SION.
SHUU
I'M SURE YOU DON'T WANT TO BE HURT ANY MORE RIGHT NOW.

DAMN YOU. ALL EVERYBODY TALKS ABOUT AROUND HERE IS THAT...

Y...
...YOU BRAT...
GGGGGG
DMP
SORRY, BUT YOU'RE NOT GOING TO GET OUT OF THIS ONE UNHARMED, KID.
DAMN YOU.
GRP

SATAN!!!

BM

THUD

ARGH!!!

THAT WAS WHEN I FOUND OUT FOR THE FIRST TIME THAT THE RINGS LILY GAVE ME WERE O-PARTS... AND THAT I WAS AN O.P.T...

CLANK

I...I CAN'T BELIEVE THE AMOUNT OF SPIRIT THIS PUNK HAS...

GGGGG
BUT IT... IT'S NOTHING TO BE AFRAID OF!!

LET ME INTRODUCE YOU TO MY FIVE O-PARTS, WHICH WILL BRING DIVINE JUSTICE UPON YOU...
SHP

AS LONG AS YOU'RE WITH ME, I DON'T NEED ANYTHING ELSE.
SO HERE'S A LITTLE PEACE OFFER-ING.
YOU'RE MY...
SP

JUSTICE!!!
...HERO, BIG BROTHER...
GWOOOO

IT'S ONLY A BUNCH OF LOW RANKING O-PARTS.
WZ WZ Z
WZ
GROOOSH!!
WIND!!
FWA
GSS
SH
TMP
SHA

TP
TP
TP
TP
SPNN

EARTH IMPACT

アース・オブ・インパクト(大地の怒り)

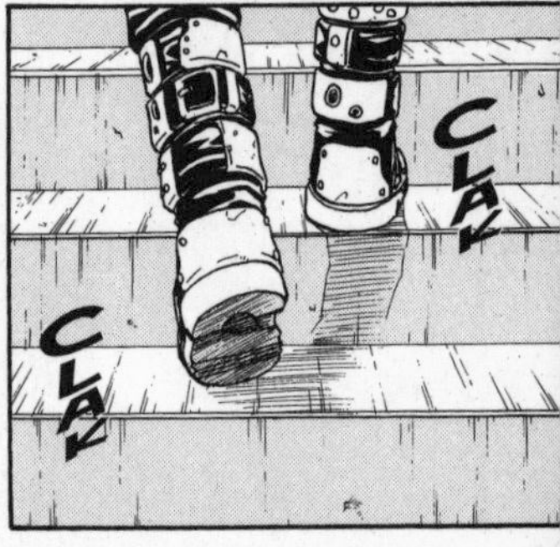
CLAK
CLAK

NICE WORK...
...COMMANDER-IN-CHIEF.

VSSSSH
PLEASE GET THE SHIP STARTED.
YES SIR.

GRP

YOU JUST WAIT, SATAN!!!

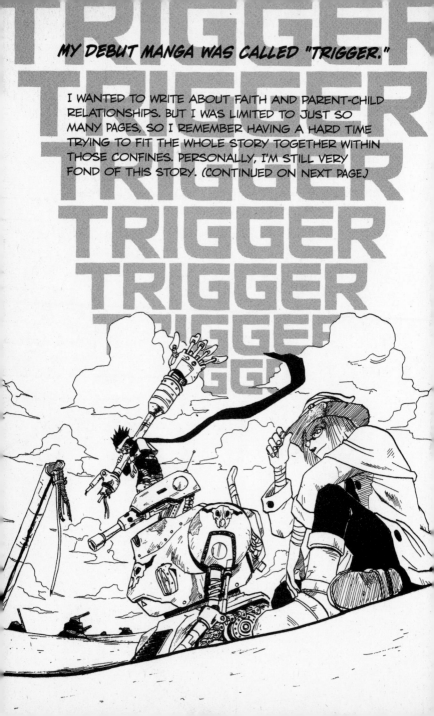

TRIGGER

TRIGGER

TRIGGER

MY DEBUT MANGA WAS CALLED "TRIGGER."

I WANTED TO WRITE ABOUT FAITH AND PARENT-CHILD RELATIONSHIPS. BUT I WAS LIMITED TO JUST SO MANY PAGES, SO I REMEMBER HAVING A HARD TIME TRYING TO FIT THE WHOLE STORY TOGETHER WITHIN THOSE CONFINES. PERSONALLY, I'M STILL VERY FOND OF THIS STORY. (CONTINUED ON NEXT PAGE.)

TRIGGER

TRIGGER

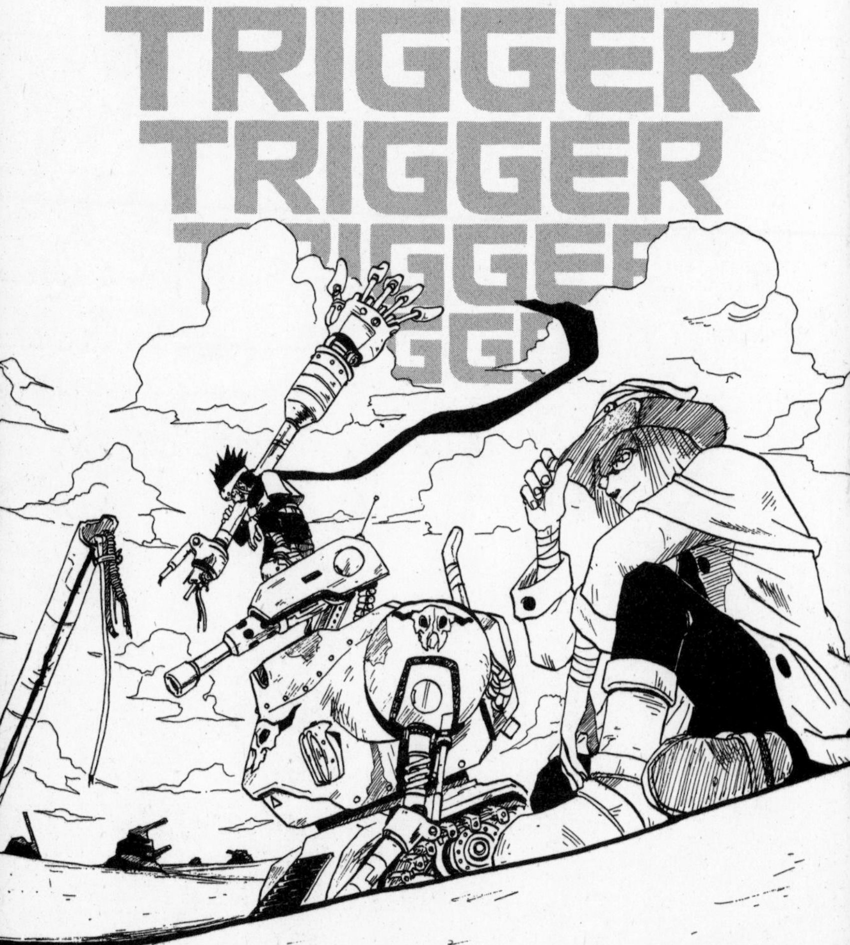

TRIGGER

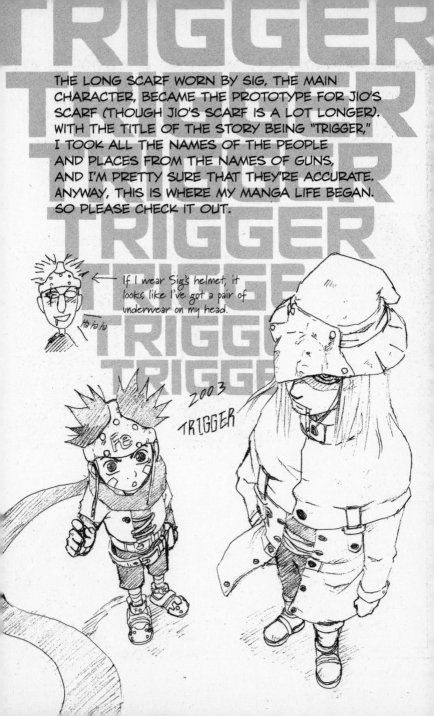

THE LONG SCARF WORN BY SIG, THE MAIN CHARACTER, BECAME THE PROTOTYPE FOR JIO'S SCARF (THOUGH JIO'S SCARF IS A LOT LONGER). WITH THE TITLE OF THE STORY BEING "TRIGGER," I TOOK ALL THE NAMES OF THE PEOPLE AND PLACES FROM THE NAMES OF GUNS, AND I'M PRETTY SURE THAT THEY'RE ACCURATE. ANYWAY, THIS IS WHERE MY MANGA LIFE BEGAN. SO PLEASE CHECK IT OUT.

If I wear Sig's helmet, it looks like I've got a pair of underwear on my head.
Ha ha ha
2003
TRIGGER
Fe

WAR CHANGES PEOPLE. THERE WAS A TIME WHEN A DEVASTATING WAR ENGULFED THE PLANET...
BOOM
GDOOOOSH
FSH
DKKKSH

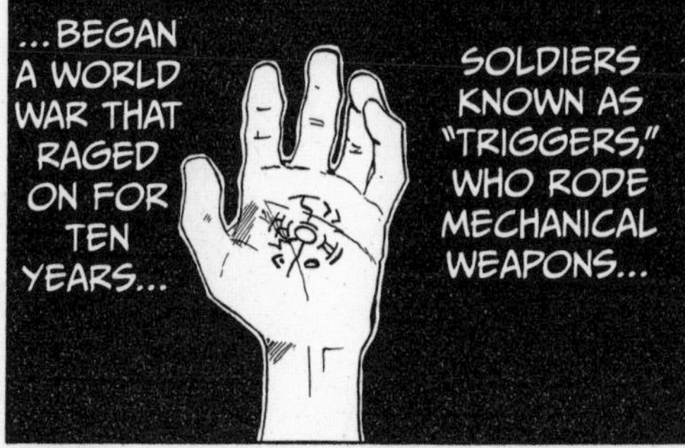
SOLDIERS KNOWN AS "TRIGGERS," WHO RODE MECHANICAL WEAPONS...
...BEGAN A WORLD WAR THAT RAGED ON FOR TEN YEARS...

...AND DESTROYED EVERYTHING. ALL SIGNS OF NATURE WERE OBLITERATED AND THE WORLD BECAME A VAST DESERT.
BUT THIS LONG WAR WAS SUDDENLY BROUGHT TO AN END WITH THE VICTORY OF THE COUNTRY OF STEA...

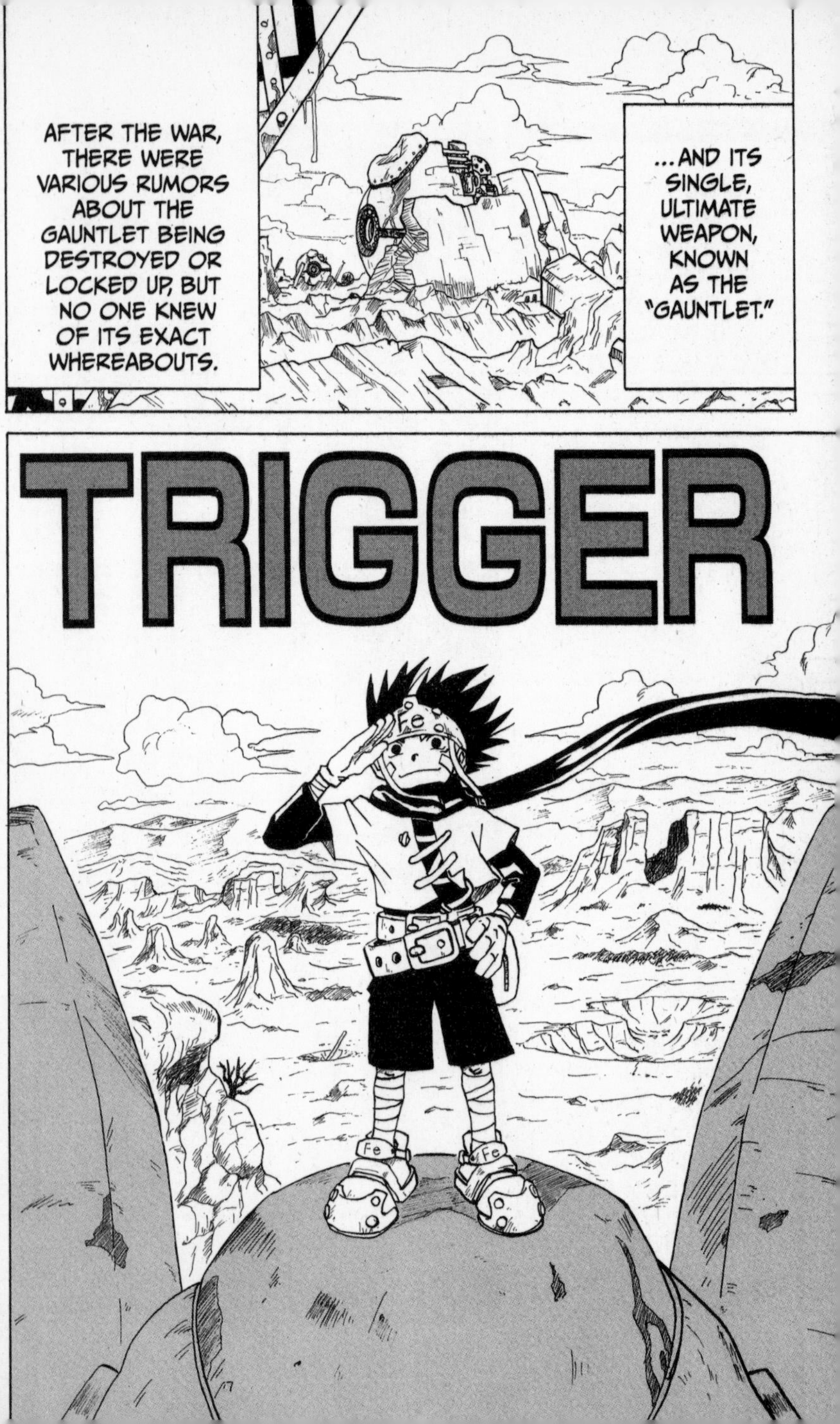

...AND ITS SINGLE, ULTIMATE WEAPON, KNOWN AS THE "GAUNTLET."
AFTER THE WAR, THERE WERE VARIOUS RUMORS ABOUT THE GAUNTLET BEING DESTROYED OR LOCKED UP, BUT NO ONE KNEW OF ITS EXACT WHEREABOUTS.

TRIGGER

THIS THING IS HUGE!!
TARIQ!!
...'CAUSE IT'S GOING TO EXPLODE!!
AND YOU'LL BE CAUGHT IN IT...
WHUP
WHUP
WHOA.
WAIT.
HEY!!
TH
OOF.
UD
HEY, SIG, DON'T GET IN THE WAY OF MY WORK!!
HURRY UP AND GET AWAY FROM IT...

SP
MMFF... MMFF... (HELP ME!)
FLAP FLAP

CLICK

D-DOOOOOM

DAMN IT!! HELP ME BEFORE YOU DETONATE THAT THING!!!
IT'S SAFER IN THE SAND. IT'S A LOT NOISIER OUT HERE.

ZCH
YOU AREN'T HURT OR ANYTHING, SO WHAT ARE YOU ANGRY ABOUT?
ZCH

HUH ?!
GRRRRR.

AAH!! NO WAY!!
OUR FIRE-BALL'S BEEN BLOWN TO PIECES!!
WHO THE HELL ARE YOU TWO?!

HUH... IT'S NOT UNCOMMON TO MEET HAS-BEEN SOLDIERS LIKE YOU GUYS THESE DAYS.
SHUT UP. WE'RE ASKING YOU WHO YOU ARE.
JUST BECAUSE YOU'VE GOT THE SKILLS TO CONTROL MACHINES THAT HAVE BEEN ABANDONED AFTER THE WAR...
...DOESN'T MEAN YOU'VE GOT THE RIGHT TO ATTACK SMALL VILLAGES...
I'M JUST A CLEANER ...
...WHO FINDS THOSE MACHINES BEFORE TRIGGERS LIKE YOU GET TO THEM AND CLEAN 'EM UP—PERMANENTLY.

DAMN YOU!!

WAIT A MINUTE. I'VE GOT A TON OF TNT BURIED RIGHT UNDER YOU GUYS.
MAKE ANY STRANGE MOVES AND IT'S BOOM WITH A PRESS OF THIS BUTTON!!

HUH!! YOU'RE JUST BLUFFING.

HEY... YOU'VE ALREADY USED IT. THEY'LL FIND OUT.

TCH. DAMN IT. LET'S GO.
WHAT ?!
THE MACHINE'S BEEN DESTROYED ANYWAY. THERE'S NO USE FIGHTING ABOUT IT.

PHEW. THAT WAS A CLOSE CALL.
THUD

WHOA, IT SURE WAS CLOSE. TOO CLOSE!!
ZSH
ZSH
FOR THEM...

HUH?! WHY?
HEH.

KABOOM
CLICK
S...SO YOU REALLY DID HAVE SOME EXPLOSIVES BURIED THERE...
HMM.
OH.
AH.
TARIQ, WAIT UP.
TP TP TP
DONE.
WHY ARE YOU ALWAYS LAGGING BEHIND ME?
IF YOU NEED TO GO TO THE BATHROOM, MAKE SURE YOU HIDE BEHIND SOMETHING. HA HA.
HUFF
HUFF
HMPH
THAT'S NOT IT.
LET'S GO BACK TO TOWN AND EAT.
I'M HUNGRY.
I INTEND TO DO THAT.
HMPH.

HERE'S THE MONEY!!
THD
CAN'T YOU GIVE ME A LITTLE MORE?
YOU'RE GONNA HAVE TO GET RID OF A BIGGER MACHINE IF YOU WANT MORE.
STOP JOKING.
THE ONE YOU DESTROYED WAS A REALLY OLD-FASHIONED MODEL.
TRIGGER
TRIGGER
YOU TWO BETTER BE CAREFUL...
...THERE'S A RUMOR THAT ANOTHER TRIGGER'S PRETTY CLOSE BY.

WELL, THIS TOWN'S SURROUNDED BY MOUNTAINS, SO IT WON'T BE THAT EASY TO FIND.
YOU'VE GOT A CUTE KID WITH YOU, SO I'D ADVISE YOU TO STOP THIS CLEANING BUSINESS.
YOU'RE MAKING A MISTAKE. THIS ISN'T MY SON.
OH, THEN YOU'RE SINGLE?!
ARE YOU FREE TONIGHT?
...

HERE.
CLATTER
CLATTER

HUH?

YOU'VE GOT FOOD ALL OVER YOUR FACE.
WIP
WIP
IT'S OKAY, DAD.

FOR GOD'S SAKE.
WIP
WIP
HA HA.

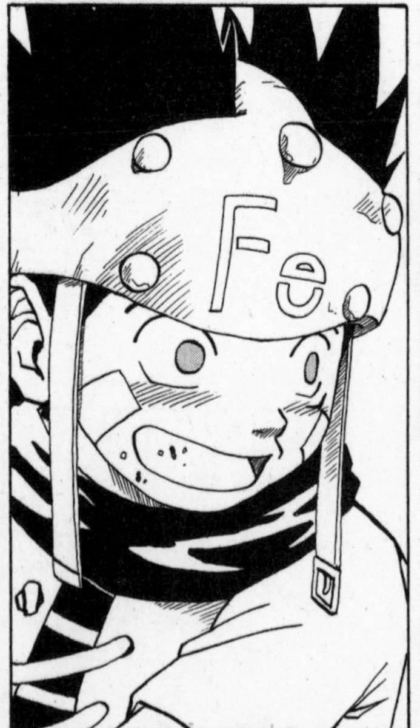

SLLRP
SLLRP
CHILD

HEY, TARIQ.
HUH ?!
CHILD

WHAT'S TAKING YOU SO LONG? HURRY UP AND EAT YOUR FOOD.
MUNCH
MUNCH

TARIQ
...
...YOU
IDIOT...!!

HE'S GONE TO BED AT LAST.
ZZZ ZZZ
ZZZ ZZZ
HEY!!
ANSWER ME IF YOU'RE ALIVE. STOP SLEEPING WITH THAT SMIRK ON YOUR FACE.
TAKING A NAP IN THE MIDDLE OF A DESERT ISN'T FUNNY, YOU KNOW.
WHOA!! HE WOKE UP!
HUH?! WHO ARE YOU...
MURF
SNIFF
I THOUGHT I TOLD YOU GOOD-BYE AT THE LAST VILLAGE.
STOP FOLLOW-ING ME.
ZLSH ZLSH

AAAAAAAH!! WHAT'S THAT?!
ACK
!
HUH?
SWOOOSH
HUFF
HUFF
HUFF
HE WON'T FIND ME NOW.
TAP
TAP
WHOA.
WHOA.
WHOA... I WAS JUST JOKING! HA HA.
PWOOSH
Y... YOU...
MY NAME? YOU WANT TO KNOW MY NAME?!
MY NAME'S SIG!!

ZZZ

ZZZ
SIG.

GOOD NIGHT.
CLICK

HAA...

WE'VE GOT TROUBLE!! TARIQ, WE'VE SPOTTED ANOTHER TRIGGER!!
SLAM
IT'S RIGHT AT THE TOWN'S MAIN GATE! COULD YOU...

HE'S GONE !!
HE'S GONE !!
HUH? HUH?
TARIQ? COME ON, YOU'VE GOT TO BE JOKING!! ONLY THE KID'S HERE!!

PWINK
HUH?
!!
DOOOM
RX-407

BUILDING A TOWN INSIDE A MOUNTAIN...
SNIK SNIK
...IS A GOOD IDEA. THE PEOPLE HERE ARE PRETTY SHARP, BUT...

HUH?
OH, HELLO HANDSOME!!

WAIT A MINUTE !!!
THIS GUY!!

HE'S GONE.
HE'S GONE.
HE'S GONE.
HE'S GONE.

TARIQ'S GONE!! HE LEFT ME AGAIN! DAMN IT!! FOR GOD'S SAKE!!!

I...I KNEW IT. DAMN IT... HE DOESN'T LIKE ME...

I'LL NEVER BE ABLE TO FIND ANYBODY WHO REALLY TRUSTS ME...

I'VE HAD ENOUGH OF HIM!! DAMN!!!
TM

BUT...BUT BEFORE I GO, I'M GOING TO GIVE HIM A PIECE OF MY MIND!!!

BRAW
BRAW
BRAK
DSH DSH DSH
WHAP
URGH!

TARIQ !!
TARIQ !!
TARIQ !!
TP TP TP
TCH... THAT IDIOT.

WHY DO YOU KEEP FOLLOW-ING ME?!!
HOW STUPID CAN YOU BE?!

BM
DON'T YOU GET IT?!
I...
WHOA.

...HATE HAVING YOU WITH ME!!!
B-BMP
JUST GO AWAY!!

YOU HAVEN'T CHANGED AT ALL. YOU'RE STILL A REAL MEANIE.
CHMP
THAT VOICE... IT CAN'T BE!!!
LONG TIME NO SEE... ♡

...CAPTAIN TARIQ.

GLOCK!!!

DAMN YOU!! HAVE YOU FORGOTTEN ABOUT THE OATH WE MADE?!

TO HAVE HONOR AS A MEMBER OF STEA'S TRIGGER FORCE!!!

SNIK SNIK

FOOL. THE TRIGGER FORCE IS MADE UP OF ELITE SOLDIERS WHO HAVE THE SKILLS TO CONTROL ANY WEAPON THAT EXISTS.

ANYBODY WHO DOESN'T PUT THOSE SKILLS TO USE IN THIS DAMNED WORLD IS AN IDIOT.

MY SKILLS ARE FAR BETTER THAN THEY USED TO BE.

I'M SURE I'M EVEN ABLE TO CONTROL STEA'S "ULTIMATE WEAPON."

SNIK SNIK

I INTEND TO FIND IT AT ALL COSTS. ALL WE DID WAS FIGHT FOR OUR COUNTRY, BUT AFTER THE WAR, PEOPLE BEGAN TO TREAT US LIKE DIRT...

SO ONCE I FIND IT, I'M GOING TO GET MY REVENGE, AND KILL THEM ALL.

HA HA HA HA HA HA!

THE LEGENDARY TRIGGER, HUH? THAT'S A GOOD ONE. *HA HA HA.*

WHA... WHAT'S WRONG, TARIQ? WHY ARE YOU LAUGHING?

I KILLED THEM...

HUH?

KILLED THEM?

WHAT'S THERE TO THINK ABOUT? IT'S EASY—YOU JUST HAVE TO BETRAY THAT KID LIKE YOU DID YOUR FAMILY BEFORE...

VWRRRR

TARIQ...

HA HA
HA HA.
HA HA
HA HA.

YOU DID THAT, DIDN'T YOU, SIG?!!

STOP FOLLOW-ING ME!!

Fe
HEY, TARIQ!!

TA-DAH
HEY, DAD!! LOOK AT ME.
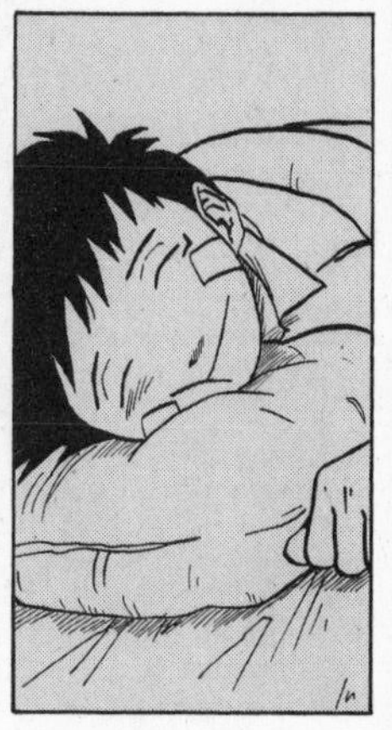

HOW MANY TIMES DO I HAVE TO TELL YOU...

GO AWAY!!! I SAID ...
...I HATED YOU, DIDN'T I?!!

B-BMP

LEER
HUH, I'VE GOT NO INTENTION OF LETTING EITHER OF YOU GO ANYWAY!!
FROM NOW ON, I'M—
THE LEGEND-ARY TRIGGER!!!
BRAK BRAK BRAK BRAK BRAK
DIE!!!
THD THD THD THD
THD THD THD THD
DIE!!!
DIE!!!
BRAK BRAK BRAK BRAK
HA HA HA! THEY'RE BULLET-RIDDLED FOR GOOD!
SHUUU
WSH WSH

HUH?
Fe
DOOM
CLONK
Fe

I UNDERSTAND NOW.

...THOSE WHO ARE PRECIOUS TO ME...
WHAP
SNIK
SNIK
BSHOOOO
SHK
SHK

RAAAAP

PING DING

BRAKAKAKAK

AAAAAAAH!!!

BOM

AND I'LL NEVER...

...BECOME A TOOL OF WAR AGAIN!!!

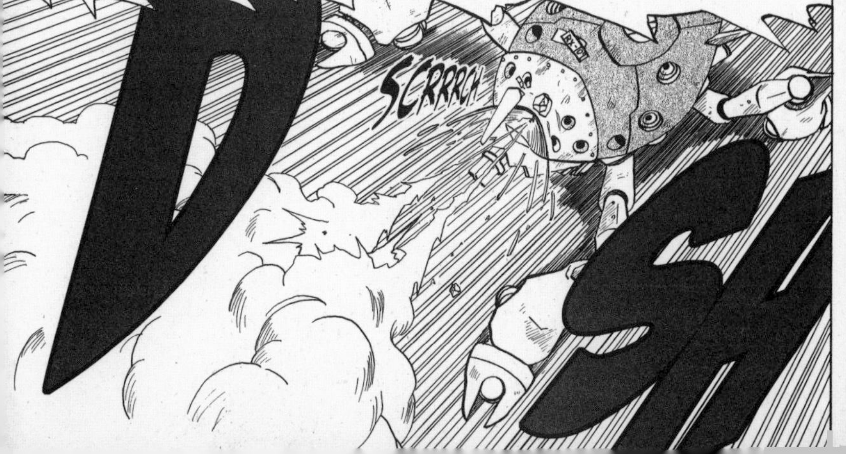

FSH
H...HE PIERCED ITS ARMOR!!!
HE'S LIKE A LIVING BULLET!!!
A... LIVING BULLET ...?!

THE STEA ARMY SAID THEY FAILED TO CREATE A HUMANOID TYPE...
BUT HE DESTROYED THIS RX-107... S...SO... THIS KID IS...

DOO
OSH
FORMER ULTIMATE WEAPON OF STEA...
SIG GAUNTLET!!
GUYS LIKE YOU...WILL NEVER BE ABLE TO PULL MY TRIGGER.

ALL I EVER SAW WAS FIRE, SCRAPS OF METAL AND DEAD PEOPLE...
AND I TOOK THAT FOR GRANTED. THE WAY THE SCIENTISTS LOOKED AT ME... I WAS ALWAYS ALONE. AND I FOUND OUT...

...THAT I WASN'T HUMAN. JUST A TOOL...

BUT I ESCAPED FROM THE LABORATORY AND MET TARIQ.
HUH?

IT WAS THE FIRST TIME ANY-BODY HAD LOOKED AT ME WITH KIND EYES.
I STILL CAN'T BELIEVE...
...THAT YOU'RE THE ULTIMATE WEAPON.

FORGIVE ME, SIG. I WAS AFRAID THAT I'D BETRAY THE PEOPLE WHO LOVED ME AGAIN...
I GUESS I DIDN'T EVEN BELIEVE IN MYSELF.

BACK THEN...

I ONLY HEARD YOU SAY THAT YOU LIKED ME, TARIQ.
...IT SOUNDED LIKE YOU SAID YOU LIKED ME.

I'VE ALWAYS WANTED TO ASK...
WHAT IS IT THAT YOU'RE DOING... EVERY TIME I FINISH A JOB?
HUH?
HA HA HA.
IT'S NOTHING. DON'T WORRY ABOUT IT. JUST HURRY UP AND GET BETTER...
..."DAD."
WH... WHAT DID YOU JUST CALL ME?!
FINE, I'LL NEVER SAY THAT AGAIN.
I HAVE...
...FAITH ...
TRIGGER / THE END

SEISHI AND SODA

SEISHI AND THE HAIR DRYER

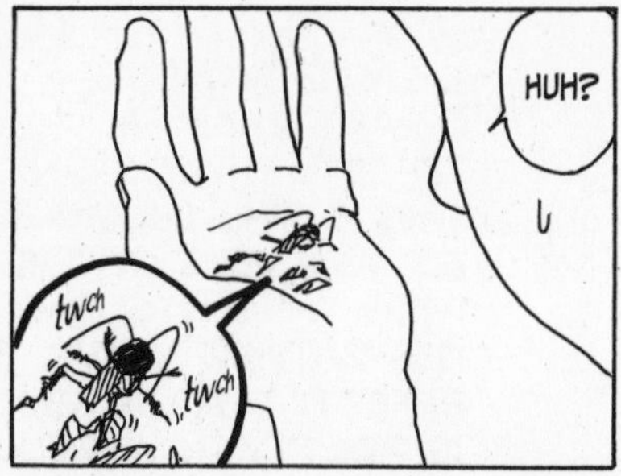

※These four-panel manga are nonfiction.

O-Parts CATALOGUE⑥

O-PART: BOMBER
O-PART RANK: B
EFFECT: EXPLOSION
THIS IS THE B-RANKED O-PART THAT ALL 50 MEMBERS OF THE UBO CLAN CARRY WITH THEM. ITS ONLY DRAWBACK IS THAT IT'S RATHER HEAVY, BUT IT IS HIGHLY EFFECTIVE AS A WEAPON AND ITS EFFECT IS PRETTY POWERFUL TOO. IF YOU GET SUPER BUFFED UP AND MACHO LIKE THE UBO CLAN, IT CAN BE A VERY EFFECTIVE O-PART.

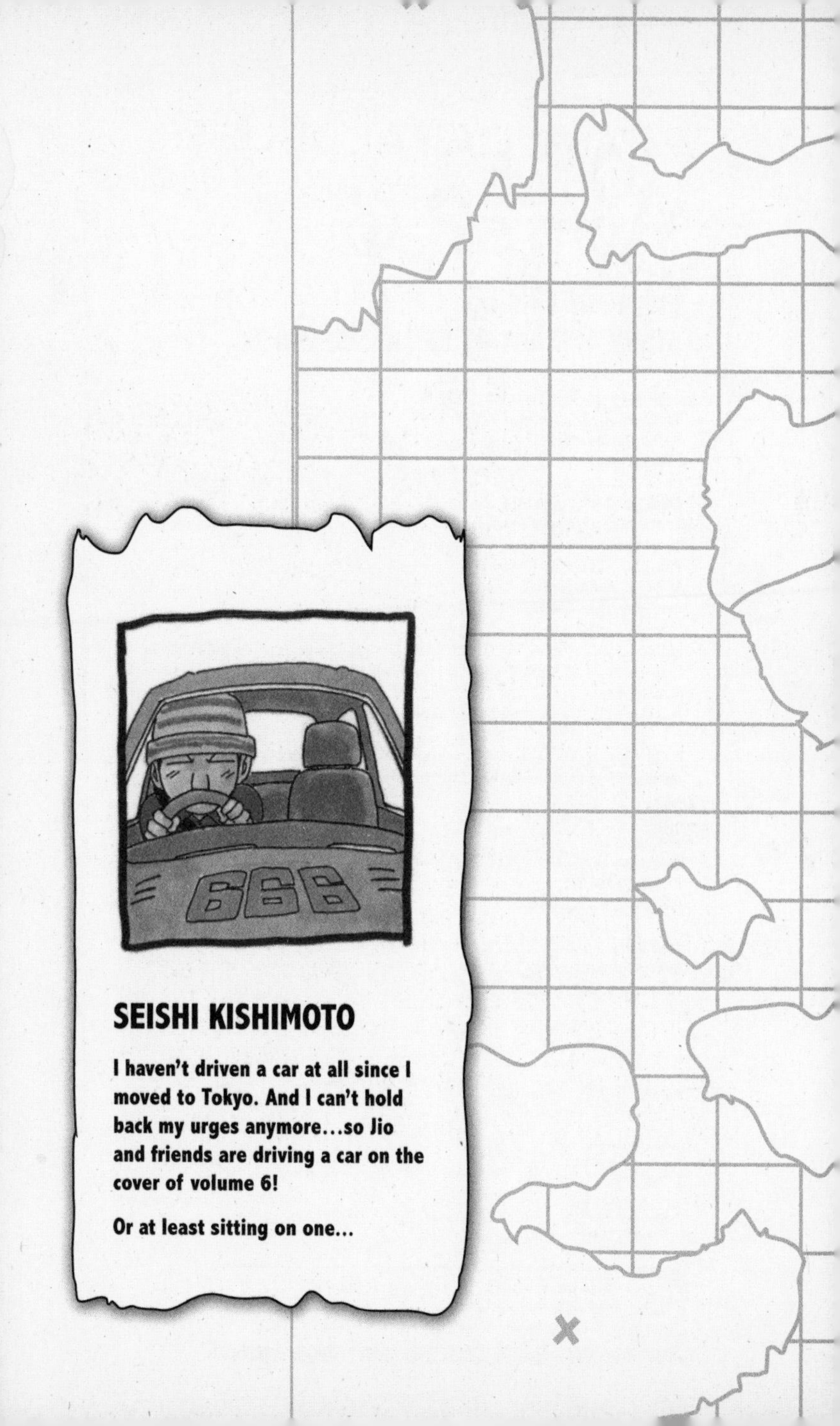

SEISHI KISHIMOTO

I haven't driven a car at all since I moved to Tokyo. And I can't hold back my urges anymore...so Jio and friends are driving a car on the cover of volume 6!

Or at least sitting on one...

VIZ Media Edition
STORY AND ART BY SEISHI KISHIMOTO

English Adaptation/Tetsuichiro Miyaki
Touch-up Art & Lettering/Gia Cam Luc
Design/Andrea Rice
Editor/Carol Fox

Editor in Chief, Books/Alvin Lu
Editor in Chief, Magazines/Marc Weidenbaum
VP of Publishing Licensing/Rika Inouye
VP of Sales/Gonzalo Ferreyra
Sr. VP of Marketing/Liza Coppola
Publisher/Hyoe Narita

Printed in the U.S.A.

Published by VIZ Media, LLC
P.O. Box 77010
San Francisco, CA 94107

10 9 8 7 6 5 4 3 2
First printing, October 2007
Second printing, January 2008

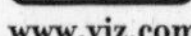

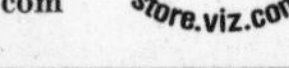

PARENTAL ADVISORY
O-PARTS HUNTER is rated T+ for Older Teen and is recommended for ages 16 and up. This volume contains realistic and fantasy violence and adult situations.

ratings.viz.com